ISBN-13: 9781478336730

ISBN-10: 1478336730

The Spirits of Birds, Bears, Butterflies and All Those Other Wild Creatures

By Thomas "Dennie" Williams

PUBLISHED BY

Thomas "Dennie" Williams for CreateSpace

The Spirits of Birds, Bears, Butterflies and All Those
    Other Wild Creatures

This book is a work of non-fiction. The characters are real and identified. The contents have been carefully investigated for accuracy.

Reading Material Suited for All Ages, But Particularly Young Adults.

Many thanks for the editorial support by Dr. John Briggs, professor of Writing, Linguistics, and Creative Process at Western Connecticut State University, who read parts of the book to help me evaluate its further needs.

The beliefs of the author, reflected in this book, are reflected in this passage.

"Spirituality is: listening to the birds singing deep in the woods near the rush of a river; smelling the purple lilacs in bloom in bushes surrounding you; staring at a bright yellow half moon's face in dark blue skies; tasting a ripe wild blackberry in the midst of its bush; or touching the nose of a friendly dolphin as it surfaces from the ocean adjacent to a sail boat. But, spirituality's arousing, inspiring, supernatural experiences surface regularly only with experienced and appreciative humans. They are only those with natural environmental instincts, joy in viewing beauty in the wild, and sensitivity to all of the sights, smells, tastes, feelings and sounds emitted by every wild creature and plant. Once such human spirit becomes a habit, it is a power equal to or beyond even the kindest, noblest religious belief: indeed, because that spirited instinct is within the heart of most all those living, dwelling or growing closest to the earth. Unfortunately, it is not a common trait for all humans. If it was, we would be living in peace, without wars. Do wild creatures create battles to wantonly kill other beings like humans do? No! Do they kill for reasons other than food nourishment? If they do, those rare beasts are either crazed, protecting their family, or out of the ordinary man eaters."

Table of Contents and Chapter Summaries

Prologue: The tale explaining how the author grew up among family who gradually influenced his deep appreciation of wildlife, and ultimately, decades later, his belief in spirits, creating the potential for interaction and communication among wildlife and people.

Introduction entitled People Believe In Communications With Pets, But Rarely Wildlife: A deeply researched explanation of how wild creatures communicate and connect with humans in all sorts of fascinating situations.

Chickadees and The Ancient Birder: A poem suggesting a floating spirit: birds' interactions – chants to the old guy who feeds them.

Blueberries, Butterflies and The Pig, explains how only at a late age, as a so called senior citizen, I finally realized there exists a spiritual, fascinating and inspiring interaction among humans and wild creatures, in this case butterflies, and people.

Butterflies, Flutterflies Hypnotize is a poetic visitation with the flying wizards.

Swallow Befriends Sailor As Almost Deadly Sea Storm Drifts Away: a potentially deadly sea turmoil rolls into an inspiring adventure when a wild flying swallow, fresh from its own dangerous mission while careening inside 48 hours of ocean winds, lands on Christopher for a relatively lengthy and friendly visit.

A Farm Boy Becomes a Spiritual Man of Nature is the story of how a country boy grew up on a Litchfield farm and as he absorbed the outdoors, wildlife, the cattle and hens, he became more and more aware of the spirits of nature.

The Saviour of Baby Wild Animals of All Kinds relates how a Connecticut woman became nurse, mother and friend to baby creatures of all kinds.

Saving Birds and Other Wildlife in The Gulf of Mexico, A Spiritual Transformation tells the tales of two bird and wild creature rescuers in the aftermath of the BP oil explosion.

The Black Bears Repeatedly Raid Bird Feeders: A personal anecdote of confrontations with Black Bears and how they relate to similar experiences of others.

The Squirrel Roams hatches descriptions of how the nutty creature roams, eats, plays and occasionally stays home with the kids.

The Great White Hunter: A humorous narration by the author's oldest childhood buddy of his dream to become a great white hunter like Daniel Boone and how his fantasy crumbled while pursuing a squirrel.

Squirrels, The Acrobats, The Raiders, The Flying Invaders: A personal ongoing history of the author's experiences with squirrels throughout his life that eventually lead from hostility to peace and humor.

The One Time Haunting Korean Hunt: In this story, the author confesses to a once in a lifetime wildlife hunting excursion on the dangerous mine-infested border between North and South Korea. The hunt is serenaded with a loud, haunting, micro-phoned back-drop of an infamous American soldier who defected to North Korea promoting that country's alleged attributes to all who listen.

Hunters! Check It Out And Think About It: Being a Vegan Makes Sense For Humans and Grizzlies Alike: This explains what it means to people of varying philosophies, including my own, to kill wild creatures for personal needs of any kind.

The Falcon and The Great Blue Heron: Two birds show how they can communicate fear, hostility and friendliness to a doctor who turned his back yard into a vineyard.

Hawks Nesting In The City Find Tragedy and Inspire Humans as Fans and Fanatics: Two Red-tailed Hawks decide to build their nest on top of a large beautiful Eagle sculpture, a cornerstone of the roof for the historic and busy Hartford, Connecticut, Superior Court Their adventures capture the imaginations of almost everyone inhabiting or visiting the court during the summer.

Hummingbird Tea: A simple sweet water feeder attracts a throng of busy Hummingbirds eventually showing their host homeowners how to keep them happy and sociable.

The Adventures and Wild Flights of Eilish: An amazing bird adventure story about a Chilean Flamingo named Eilish who escaped a Connecticut bird sanctuary in the late fall and flew north to Ontario, Canada. There it became the focus of an intense rescue effort as winter closed in. It's saviour was a well known bird and animal rescuer who became so close to the creatures she rescued that they became her spiritual friends.

Big Daddy Swan Protects His Brood From The Road Runners: The famous annual Litchfield Road Race was the scene of a dramatic confrontation between a competitive runner and a male swan trying to protect his mate and their brood from a rush of road runners.

Awesome Birds, Frogs, Snakes, Crocs and Insects Inside The Costa Rican Jungle: A poem about a trip through a Costa Rican jungle guided by an incredible nature guide who had close interaction with birds, lizards, snakes, insects and most all jungle dwellers.

The Book's Opening!

Prologue: Family Influences Bird Love

Ever since I was a wee lad, I have had bird feeders nailed to my window, hanging from tree branches or attached to poles in the yard of my two longest standing Litchfield, Connecticut, homes. All varieties of birds, including scores of Chickadees, eventually appeared on seemingly every tree branch in those wooded yards. They anxiously awaited flight dives to feeders or an ever-present suet ball inside a small, square wire cage attached to a tree branch.

Even now, on a sunny morning or afternoon, five or six varying bird calls or songs are flowing through the air constantly all around the house. Flocks of crows, guarded by a sentinel crow, perched on a high tree branch above, fly down in small groups. They meet up with other crow gangs already landed or readying to do so in a big farmed field across from our home. It's a crow convention! Caw, caw, caw, caw! That's one of their constant refrains as they creep and flap around the field in groups.

There are many variations of this common communication when they speak to one another. But, heaven forbid the noise and varying take off flying angles, if they spot a hawk!

Up, up, up goes the whole flock to catch up to that swooping hawk. They then constantly crow scream and dive individually at that big winged bird until it disappears into new territory, or finds a dense tree perch.

From time to time, those same crows visit our back yard, land on the grass, walk around, like old time war veterans, bobbing heads and pecking the ground for food. They eat almost anything: bugs, seeds, crumbs or accidentally dropped food-garbage. They love wing-flapping attacks on hanging suet balls. Multiple loud crow sounds can be annoying. But, if you watch two or three of them converse with one another close up, they are almost as funny as old Maine seamen gabbing ocean gossip.

More haunting than crow flock calls, however, are the early-morning or late-afternoon sounds of flocks Red-winged Black Birds, as they perch high up in leave-less black tree branches. It's a continuous chorus of seemingly never ending high screeches. Listen to it on YouTube! Don't miss it! (Footnote one) These and other birds flock together, the theory goes, because they want to protect themselves from predators like hawks; and they have more eyes, not only to spot that threat, but to find food. When the high pitches stop, the black birds with bright red or orange wing shoulders, break up in flocks, and fly back into their swamp grounds next to Butternut Brook, diagonally across a big corn field from our home.

That abode is a three-story, charming, colonial, vintage yellow saltbox.

"The Miss Rebecca Osborn House on Harris Plain was built in the summer of 1776. When all the great timbers were in place, the master builder (Rebecca's father, John), climbed onto the ridge pole with a bottle of rum. Standing near the west gable, he sprinkled its contents over the timber, then tossing down as far as he could to the west, shouted to the crowd below: 'Three cheers and God Save Our Country,'" says the March 8, 1906, Litchfield Enquirer. It goes on to explain that Rebecca lived in the house for nearly a century after being born in 1801.

Rebecca's old house was later sold to my mother's ancestors, the Ripley family. So, only two family clans have lived in it for well over two centuries. It is adjacent to a country road, two huge former cow roving fields, and two branches of that tiny Butternut Brook. A small lawn, gardens, a separate diminutive cow pasture and trees surround it. Four bird feeders and a suet ball lure in all varieties of feathered flier species. All neighborhood birds must feel almost like pets, since they and their relatives have frequented the area seemingly forever.

I cannot stop feeding them, and they cannot stop eating suet and sunflower seed. If the suet cage is empty, and I see woodpeckers clutching it, and sounding chit, chit, chit, guilt overwhelms me. If all seed is gone from feeders, chickadees will cry out incessantly, land repeatedly on and off the feeder or fly within feet of the house's windows. But, they most certainly are not my coquettes. They are wild and free! Nevertheless, I do regularly insist upon singing awkward, mimicking bird calls to them, mostly: "Chick-a-dee, dee, dee, dee!" Sometimes they seemingly respond particularly sparrows, catbirds or chickadees.

Bluebirds, too, with their males' sharp medium blue back and orange breast have always stirred me to grab my binoculars and catch them bobbing and weaving, as they fight to stay perched on the narrow, black telephone wire attached to the house.

The Beatles gave them their best with this sample of the melodic, lovely song's lyrics:

"Late at night when the wind is still
I'll come flying through your door
And you'll know what love is for
I'm a bluebird
I'm a bluebird, I'm a bluebird, I'm a birdbird, yeah
yeah yeah
I'm a bluebird, I'm a bluebird, I'm a birdbird, yeah
yeah yeah

Touch your lips with a magic kiss
And you'll be a bluebird too
And you'll know what love can be
I'm a bluebird
I'm a bluebird, I'm a bluebird, I'm a birdbird, yeah
yeah yeah
I'm a bluebird, I'm a bluebird, I'm a birdbird, yeah
yeah yeah

Bluebird, (Bluebird) ah ha
Bluebird, (Bluebird) ah ha
Bluebird, (Bluebird) ah ha ha

Fly away through the midnight air
As we head across the sea
And at last we will be free
You're a bluebird
You're a bluebird, you're a bluebird, you're a
bluebird, yeah yeah yeah
You're a bluebird, you're a bluebird, you're a
bluebird, yeah yeah yeah

Bluebird, (Bluebird) ah ha
Bluebird, (Bluebird) ah ha
Bluebird, (Bluebird) ah ha ha

(At last we will be free
Bluebird, like me
At last we will be free)"

(Creation credited to Paul and Lynda McCartney from MetroLyrics.com)

Through the incredible good fortune of living with a variety of wonderful characters, my immediate relatives, gradually, I developed a soul-piercing love of birds as well as all natural living wild creatures and their habitats.

One of the most enchanting influences when I was say, six or seven, was Aunt Kao, a wonderful jet-white haired, stocky, but beautiful cousin with an engaging personality. She devoted hours in the morning and late afternoon reading nature stories to my sister, Connie, and I. Auntie created each animal and bird character within a separate tone of voice. They were Thornton W. Burgess' rabbits, foxes, beavers, bears, toads, and coyotes. The characters included Peter Cottontail, a rabbit, Reddy The Fox, Jimmy Skunk and Jerry Muskrat. I remember how Peter Cottontail constantly escaped Reddy The Fox even though Reddy was so, so clever. And I remember how Danny Meadow Mouse loved the snow.

"Now Danny Meadow Mouse is a stout hearted little fellow, and when rough Brother North Wind came shouting across the Green Meadows, tearing to pieces the snow clouds and shaking out the snowflakes until they covered the Green Meadows deep, deep, deep, Danny just snuggled down in his warm coat in his snug little house of grass and waited. Danny liked the snow. Yes, sir, Danny Meadow Mouse liked the snow. He just loved to dig in it and make tunnels." That's the prose from "The Adventures of Danny Meadow Mouse," by Thornton W. Burgess, Illustrated by Harrison Cady.

It took all of seven decades for me to gradually absorb what has now become a belief: wildlife not only interacts with people, but communicates with them, most often when those human mortals have no idea it is happening. So, by habit, birds, bears and butterflies are much more conscious of intercommunications or interactions among all living beings than humans are. What convinced me of that, beyond all doubt, were two extraordinary experiences with amazingly engaging butterflies many years apart. They are the first of several short tales included later in this book.

Like my own seven decades of density before discovery, most humans have no clue whatsoever that animals, birds, fish and other creatures are capable of interplay or communications with them. For all those without a special love for wildlife, that is a crucial problem. If a human believes another living being cannot communicate, then those beings become largely intangible or irrelevant to their lives.

Loving communications engender care and consideration. Lack of human interaction with wild creatures creates impassiveness, and eventually thoughtlessness, potentially leading to negligence: like continuing to speed a car when a squirrel crosses the road. Personal attitudes or beliefs trifling wildlife create dangerous contempt for wild creatures, as well as all of nature. With all the extraordinarily devastating powers humans have, such a belief in the insignificance of wildlife, can prove and has proven malignant for the health of the world's endless natural environments.

"There are many aesthetic, spiritual, ecological, scientific, social, political, commercial, economic and recreational values associated with wildlife. The gradual disappearance of many wildlife species is a problem of large proportions and increasing urgency. Humans and wildlife share the same environments and are thus subject to many of the same environmental conditions. However, wildlife is typically more sensitive to environmental changes than are humans, and can serve as a good indicator to the overall quality of our environment," says the Environmental Education and Training Partnership. (Footnote two)

"Global Psychics believes that learning to communicate with animals and nature, connecting spiritually, from the heart is one of the first steps in developing one's psychic ability - and essential to learning to live comfortably with our environment," that Internet site says. (Footnote three)

"Animals can put us in touch with our authentic power. To communicate with them is to literally stand in the presence of love disguised in fur, feather, hoof, wing paw, and claw. They are masters in disguise. Animals anoint, bless, cleanse, and restore wholeness. They return us to the sacredness of the earth, teaching us the art of atonement," says Gina Palmer, who promotes telepathic animal communications. www.animaltalk.net

*John and Julie Forman Exploring Exotic Locales Always
With an Emphasis on Nature.. (Photographer
Unidentified)*

Two of the rare humans who taught me the language
of spirituality in nature and life were John and Julie
Forman, my maternal uncle and aunt. They were
deeply religious persons who loved hiking, horse
trail riding and tenting out in the Canadian and
Northern New England wildernesses.

They constructed two temporary summer homes deep within nature's confines: the first in a honey colored log cabin next to the Bow River in Banff, Canada; and years later, and another inside a small Barnard, Vermont, A-frame, overlooking New York's Adirondack Mountains, clear to spectacular Mt. Mansfield in faraway Stowe, Vermont.

They treated my father, mother, sister and I to lengthy visits of those homes and two or three camping, canoeing and hiking trips to Moose Head Lake in Northern Maine and Lake Louise in Banff National Park, Alberta, Canada. We experienced the exciting fun of encountering bears, moose, elk, water birds and other wildlife while country exploring, camping and canoeing.

On one horseback trip, the six of us rode several miles up a steep mountain into the breath-taking Crowfoot Glacier, twenty miles Northwest of Lake Louise. The glacier is aptly named. It has claws on its foot, like a crow. Canadian crows grow big in the fresh, cold air surrounding the glacier.

Once at the end of the trail, we dismounted and hitched up the horses. On foot, we climbed down a small sandy bank toward crystal clear water. On the edge that pristine lake, we took our folded fishing poles out of our packs and began repeatedly casting for trout.

But, within less than a half hour, the clear, blue, sunlit spring day became a sky entirely clouded over. Unexpectedly, snow began falling. Startled, we all packed up our fishing gear and quickly mounted the horses. Soon, the air was filled with a myriad of white, frosty flakes. It began to look like a near blizzard, creating a scary trip back down the mountain path to Lake Louise.

As we descended, my mischievous horse enjoyed putting its front feet together and sliding ten-to-fifteen yards down the trail through big wet, muddy snow swatches. I was frightened and yelled out alarms, but Uncle John, riding close behind, assured me the trail horses knew what they were doing. Nevertheless, my horse occasionally struck more fear into my heart by four-beat walking close to the edge of cliffs and feigning a lean toward the cliff-ledges.

Hours later, after the snow stopped and the sun returned, we did miraculously reach the bottom safely. However, my blue jeans became so shrunken from the ride, I needed help dismounting. Then, it seemingly took minutes for my bowed legs to straighten. What a relief it was to be back in the sunshine now, safe at glorious Lake Louise! That trip was an adventure, never forgotten.

As I later discovered, Julie Forman was no stranger to travel adventures. When Julie was in her twenties and unmarried, she, her brother, Louie, and my Mom, Connie, travelled, mostly by boat, from Cuba to California to Hawaii. That marked just the start for what became an ongoing adventuresome Asian trip together. Julie wrote a detailed vacation diary. This short passage, one of many diary nature descriptions, expresses excitement while driving along the Hawaiian seacoast:

"Well away we went for a motor ride over the Island, and such a ride it was. No one can describe a place. You must see it to know. First thick and feathery and green through the trees with smells of the most exotic fragrant kinds; and then crisp and blue over the views with clear cut purple crags and volcanoes and the feathery green way below you and somewhere down over the green the sea, a most transparent jewel-like sea-the likes of which you feel more than see."

In the late 1930s, during the depression, the Formans founded what became Litchfield's first co-educational private school, The Forman School. It started with 3 boys and expanded to 180 boys and girls, was founded to help free those children from learning and other disabilities. John's spiritual DNA was clear: Both of his grandfathers were missionaries in India, and one founded the Forman Christian College in Lahore, India. John's father was headmaster of a school in Gwalior, India, for Indian princes.

Here is how Julie and John Forman promoted spiritual nature as a symbol for their students. The Forman Shield, marking the school's signature and its outside sign of welcome to all, contained a Lion!

Quoting from John's 1956 commencement address comes this explanation: "The Lion stands (for) courage, which is moral courage. That lion is alert to every bold claim or trickly little suggestion of evil, and has its paw raised and its jaw open in warning that it will be rough with every evil that tries to come too close. It stands safely, because it has its back to the right. The lion---moral courage—is king of the jungle: never forget that!"

As a student without disabilities, I attended the school for a half dozen years. A student colleague of mine, Lowber Welsh, kept a pet crow on campus. It used to fraternize daily by diving low down from its perches on rooftop arches after classes ended. The big black-feathered one swooped just feet over students' and faculty members' heads repeatedly screeching: "Caw, caw, caw!" Its nest in a nearby pine tree was ultimately discovered by a student or faculty member. Its open-sticked hollow was filled with jewelry, coins and other shiny objects belonging to students, faculty, and just anyone who happened by.

In their spare time, the Formans lived in a quaint natural wood house on a steep hill overlooking Litchfield. Its three tenths of a mile driveway is so long, bumpy and angled, it is not worth plowing in heavy winter snows. As the road begins below, there is a small Beaver pond inhabited as well by fish, their predators, Blue Herons, and ducks and geese. At the top of the hill's road is the weathered clapboard structured house with a central red brick chimney, sticking out of the grey-brown shingled roof. It is tucked about fifty yards below the hill's high point to the north. It was built by John, some Forman students and a carpenter from antique wood, recovered from a barn taken down to make way for the huge Barkhamsted Reservoir in Northern Connecticut.

The house's nearby tree environs are home to Blue Birds, Barn Swallows and insect-catching Phoebes. They constantly fly around the abode and sometimes perch on the wood cow fence just outside the diminutive lawn and the house's yard from large, hilly hay fields.

Motoring a car up or down the driveway, or mowing the lawn inspires birds to fly out of the hay field with such a speed that you believe they might have never seen a car or mower before. On clear nights, we delighted in the moon, the sky filled with stars, hosts of blinking fire flies moving arbitrarily everywhere, the dimly lit forests below the hay fields, and the tiny lights of homes below.

This is the song, as sung by jazz legend Louis Armstrong, which for me creates the positive worldly spirit of John and Julie Forman:

"What A Wonderful World" (Footnote four)

"I see trees of green, red roses too
I see them bloom for me and you
And I think to myself what a wonderful world.

I see skies of blue and clouds of white
The bright blessed day, the dark sacred night
And I think to myself what a wonderful world.

The colors of the rainbow so pretty in the sky
Are also on the faces of people going by
I see friends shaking hands saying how do you do
They're really saying I love you.

I hear babies crying, I watch them grow
They'll learn much more than I'll never know
And I think to myself what a wonderful world
Yes I think to myself what a wonderful world."

My Mom and Dad and I eventually scattered the
Formans' cremation ashes in the field on the southern
front of the old homestead, overlooking a wide scope
of beautiful territory. The house's front windows
look outward toward their spirits resting places.
Step out the front door onto the lawn! The sights
below include the green way approach to beauteous
Mt. Tom Pond and the forest wilds of Prospect
Mountain. They are past countryside haunts for the
Bantam, Tunxis, Potatucks and Mohawk Indians. The
Potatuck Tribe sold some of those lands in the early
1700s to white settlers living in Hartford and
Windsor, Connecticut.

The legend says the tribe kept control over Mt. Tom Pond's forested hill directly above it. The rear window views of the quaint Forman house capture forestland and the historic Town of Litchfield, two miles distant. The spire of the Congregational Church, and beyond it, the lengthy Chestnut Hill residential neighborhood is in the background. Original colonial settlers from Hartford, Windsor and Lebanon purchased the territory around the Forman's house on the hill from the Indians.

The town was founded in 1721. During the American Revolution, it was a safe hangout for Colonial Army fighters. They gradually created it into a major route destination while regularly transporting munitions and provisions.

Living with that history for ten years helped influence my mother and father to become American antique dealers. Well known in the business for decades, they promoted and sold, among a myriad of other art, bird, animal and landscape paintings that fascinated me. Mom had been a costume designer on Broadway when she met my Dad, a salesman, through their closest of friends.

My older generational cousin, Danah B. Lowe, an accomplished, amateur short story writer, whom we affectionately called Aunt Danah, was inspired by John and Julie Forman's spirituality and their beauteous nature hide-away.

"The house on the hill was built to be hidden," Danah wrote. "Something about it is almost sacred, filled with the memory and tradition of the couple who built it. This was their escape…the house was supposed to be a small English cottage, and I am sure if there had been a way to thatch the roof, they would have done it. It is hard to imagine a more perfect and impenetrable retreat. The road, once the gate is open, is steep, full of ruts and surprising humps and rocks. At the top of the hill, there is another gate, fastened by a chain attached to a shaky pole. All of this makes for a difficult approach, especially when there are cows standing in the middle of the road. They add a certain rustic charm, and are the reason for the tight security."

The ever charming house on the hill overlooks most of the historic Town of Litchfield which was founded in 1721 and created as the county seat thirty years later. (Photo by Dennie Williams)

After her husband, John, passed away, Julie regularly visited our home at that time, a mile below her own hillside dwelling. The latter former log cabin abode, inside tall pinewoods, she ultimately gave to my wife, two children and I.

Julie, once an aspiring opera singer and an accordion player, had a musical personality. At the Forman School, she was famous with students and faculty alike for striding around campus whistling and humming songs. She loved birds of all kinds.

Each time Julie paid us a call, she walked up a long path and whistled a melody. "Here comes Aunt Julie!" exclaimed Ina, my wife, Tommie and Gisela, our two children, or myself every time one of us heard her coming.

When Julie too sadly passed on some years later, I began to notice songs, flight patterns and nest collecting activities of a pair of Cardinals. They had a tree nest nearby. That Cardinal pair never seemed to leave our pine forest from year to year. I always believed their songs and calls were a reflection of the spirits of Julie and John.

"What-cheer cheer cheer" and "whoit whoit whoit" and "birdy birdy birdy" are their song imitations, according to renditions in Peterson's Field Guide to Birds. I always keep that guide and my bird binoculars handy under the dinning room window, looking out on one of the bird feeders. They are essential for in house flight sightings and bird walks.

Always, as a child, when I explored in the woodlands or fields with my Uncle Dillon Ripley, an ornithologist, we heard all varieties of birds singing in the wetlands, woodlands and fields. Immediately after those songs, he looked at me, expectantly, to identify each of the songsters. Mostly, embarrassed, I either demurred or guessed and misidentified the songbirds or hawks or geese! That eventually convinced me to purchase the bird guide. As an extra incentive, my uncle gave me bird song audiotapes. Unfortunately, I never memorized them!

After constructing a pond and bird sanctuary as a young man, Dillon became head of Yale University's Peabody Museum of Natural History, featuring a wide variety of nature's creatures and their historical contexts. Years later, he moved on to become secretary or 'top bird' at The Smithsonian Institution, the nation's premiere science, nature, art and historical repositories.

Uncle Dillon Ripley smiles while amidst his feathered friends. (Photo from Livingston Ripley Waterfowl Conservancy)

Having that pair of Cardinals, singing songs regularly near our log cabin, was haunting, a brisk high beautiful: chip-chip-chip-chip-chip and then another and sometimes another. Most early mornings and late afternoons, they air-scurried through pine branches, perched on one for a minute or so, chirped for a few seconds, flew off and disappeared.

Later, as earlier mentioned that my soul had soon insisted, I repeatedly and earnestly told my family that the scarlet male or pinkish brown female with crested faces and the black circle, covering their eyes and surrounding their orange beak, are the spirits of John and Julie.

"I too will die," I always added dramatically, "and will return to earth as a Cardinal!" Ultimately, I felt the urge to purchase a St. Louis Cardinal baseball hat with a male Cardinal's bright red face and jet black mustache on its crest. I did that with slight hesitation because I am a life long New York Giants, and later, when they moved to the West Coast, a San Francisco Giants fan. When anyone asks whether I am a Cardinal's fan, I reply, "Actually, I am a fan of the Cardinal, the bird!"

After my immediate family moved in 1994 to my mother and father's ancient saltbox, just down the road from the log cabin, Cardinals have followed. Believe it! Some years, I've spotted at least seven pairs of the people-shy, and usually not so readily available, Cardinals, constantly feeding at the four bird feeders in our yard. In all four seasons of the year, they sing and hop all over the ground, also frequenting every bush and tree nearby.

Occasional visiting bird lovers cannot believe it! Once in a snowy winter, I spotted five of the red males perched on the branches of one five-foot tall, bare bush. It appeared to be a bird-ornamented Christmas tree. Because the females are buff brown with pink tones, they are harder to spot. They too fly all over the yard, year around. Males and females are inseparable. While I was living in that same house for 20 years as a child and young adult, I never, ever, observed more than a Cardinal pair or two.

"Hmmmm!" Again I wonder: Are some of those feathered ones the spirits of Julie and John; or my mother and father, Constance and Thomas Williams; or my Uncle and Aunt, Dillon and Mary Ripley, bird lovers all, who all have since passed away? Indeed, the Cardinals buoyant spirits sure make me feel, at least superficially, like my family members' spirits never left! Perhaps one of those Cardinal pairs also are the ghosts of Dottie and Louie Ripley, my other aunt and uncle also on my mother's side of the family They operated a small Brown Swiss cattle farm directly adjacent to this old, 1776 salt box home of ours. They cared for all kinds of animals and birds including cows, horses and chickens. Farming, although not critical to their livelihood, was a lifelong love. Horses were among Dottie's favorite living creatures. She rode them like a pro everywhere, including horse shows.

One of Dottie's favorite stories about animals relates to her close friend, Goldie, otherwise known as Margaret Wise Brown, Godmother to Laurel R. Galloway, Dottie's eldest daughter.

Here is the tale, right out of 'the horse's mouth:

I remember a cold November night when (my great friend) Goldie (a writer) came to stay with us in Litchfield. We had a dairy farm then with some beautiful fawn colored quiet Swiss cows. She had been thinking of doing a story of a barn at night. She needed to live it to find the feeling of being there in the dark with the animals. After wrapping her up in a huge coonskin coat and boots, we walked her to the barn in the sparkling cold and bedded her down in a pile of sweet smelling clover hay.

Goldie stretched out in the manger in front of a line of curious cows with big noses. They sniffed her and blew on her with their hot, silage breath. It must have been a long night!

By 5 a.m., Tony Baldi, who had worked on the place for forty years, flicked on the lights as usual and began forking out the remaining hay in the mangers. Tony was an indelible character right out of such children's stories as Dawn Bab Prochovnic's Famous Fenton Has a Farm: Sign Language for Farm Animals. He lived haying, milking, shovelling cow pies and talking to any living being that walked. He was so kind and friendly you had to love him on sight! He was a short balding guy with Italian in his blood and a laugh in his heart.

As Tony walked into the barn that early morning, suddenly he hit the biggest coon he would ever live to see, jumping back in instant terror, a tussled face appeared. "Miss Brown! Are you all right? Why are you sleeping in the manger? Did they throw you out of the house?"

Poor Tony never did understand. He helped her up, put her in the truck and off they went to his house. There they both had black coffee and a large shot of whiskey to recuperate.

The whole family was up and waiting when Goldie finally appeared. Smelling like a barn and fluffing the last bits of clover out of her blonde hair, she simply exclaimed: "Wow!" I could never write a children's story about the barn at night. Two cats slept on my fur coat and purred in my ear. The cows made endless digestive noises all night, punctuated by splashing sounds like a bad dream of Niagara Falls. The best part was seeing Tony's face when he forked the hay off a big coon that was trying to sleep in the manger.

It is a shame that Dottie, a wonderful artist, did not accompany this little tale with her artistic sketches!

My mother and I once discovered and helped Dottie put a winter fire out in an attic of that same neighboring cattle barn. At the time, most of the cows were inside trying their best to feed at their troughs. We were so anxious to put out the fire; we totally forgot they were there, right in front of us. In fact, as Aunt Dottie, my mother and I worked furiously to find and climb upwards to the smouldering blaze to put it out, "Shorty," then the Ripley's farm hand, rushed in from his nearby home below. He shyly approached within feet of his boss, Mrs. Ripley, and whispered low, but frantically:

"Mssss Ripley! The cattle are coughing! We should let them outside!" Indeed, Shorty unshackled them all, and once they backed out of their stalls, the groaning cattle rushed through the big barn door into the freezing open clear air of winter.

"Mooooooooooooo!" they all cried repeatedly with a higher sound than normal. What a relief! Ha! I know what that change in cow's sound from the norm means! As I said earlier, I KNOW my immediate family members have come back as Cardinals! Now you know I'm crazy! But I love craziness like that! Crazy like a fox bird! As I get older, I continue to whistle at and talk to those red crowned male and buff brown and pink crowned female birds all the time! Like humming along the jazz greats like Louis Armstrong and Miles Davis, it keeps me sane!

Footnote one: YouTube
http://www.youtube.com/watch?v=otjmIpbF68

Footnote two: Environmental Education and Training Partnership
http://eelink.net/eetap/info114.pdf

Footnote three: Global Psychics
http://www.globalpsychics.com/category/animal-communications/

Footnote four: Song Writers are Bob Thiele, George David Weiss and George Douglas
http://ask.yahoo.com/20030804.html

Introduction - People Believe In Communications With Pets But Rarely Wildlife

"A man is ethical only when life, as such, is sacred to him, and that of plants and animals, as that of his fellowmen, and when he devotes himself helpfully to all life that is in need of help, says "Out of My Life and Thought," an autobiographical epilogue by Albert Schweitzer.

Worldwide men, women and children talk incessantly to pets. Dogs, cats, caged birds, tanked fish, and even snakes, absorb endless human talk, petting and other imaginative forms of communication. But, do human beings actually listen to their pets' spirits or inner sensibilities? Do they understand them? Maybe! Maybe not is more likely for many, including myself in the olden days when my immediate family hosted pet dogs and cats.

People are obsessed with possessing animals and loving them, sometimes with intensity almost beyond the powers of imagination. They dress them up in ridiculously fancy vests, hats, neck chains and ribbons. Once in a while, they feed them into obesity. They sleep in the same bed with them. They put them in fish tanks, cages and fenced in fields. Yet most living creatures instinctively crave freedom, and live more naturally and relaxed with as much of it as they can get. I must add, however, that some dogs become so attached to their masters, they begin acting more and more like humans. They are either so calm their barks disappear, or so protective or angry, they bark or show their teeth incessantly at strangers walking nearby.

As kind as some people are to animals, birds, fish and other living creatures, they have to think more about those creatures' innate desires for freedom and independence. And, above all, humans need constant empathy for wild animals, birds and all other untamed critters. If more of them expressed such kindness, nature could flourish in wider areas worldwide and man-made pollution disasters might decrease in kind. Can you imagine poisoning, torturing or intentionally running over a rabbit, squirrel, deer or roadside crow? I can't!

But, I must confess, I did run over a wild creature once or twice accidentally. I know a squirrel ran into the path of my car once or twice. That was indeed upsetting, however, the experience was not nearly as bad as an incident I still remember vividly with horror more than 50 years after it occurred.

It was late in the afternoon as the sun began to set. Then a college student, I was driving in my first car ever on Vermont's often steep Route 125 back to Middlebury College, 13 miles away.

I had been skiing most of the day at the college's Snow Bowl. My grandmother, Constance B. Ripley, gave me her car, an old green Mercury sedan. It was so rounded my college buddies and I joked that it looked like an upside down bathtub. Of course, 'gran' told me drive safely always, and avoid any potential accidents.

That day, as I drove down a slight slope, probably too fast, I spotted a large fawn crossing the road, immediately in front of me. I made exasperating noises, hit the break hard and flew a bit sideways in the sedan. But horrifyingly I heard the fawn hit the bumper as I was skidding to a stop. I shoved open the door and jumped out. Immediately, I saw the fawn's back leg was broken. It was hobbling and dragging itself back toward an adjacent deep snow covered field from the middle of the road. I was crying with terror at the sight. Worse yet! I could see the miniature one would not survive. Within seconds, I knew I must take the youngster out of its misery. But, I had never, ever done such a thing.

So I rushed to a stone wall nearby, grabbed a rock, ran over to the fawn and threw the rock repeatedly at its head until it died. I was constantly yelling and crying. Then, I dragged the fawn by its front feet off the road and into the bushes. When I drove back to college, I confessed to negligent driving and that mercy killing to classmates.

I don't understand! How can countless hunters joyfully and repeatedly kill endangered wild creatures, sometimes even in national parks where no hunting is allowed? How do corporations, operated by people, endlessly pollute the air, water and earth where wildlife lives and where wildlife will slowly die from those human poisons?

With humans, the tendency is to talk at pets, and then create their own dreamed up answers back. It is identical to superficial conversations among human families. Within easy hearing range, someone says something clear and elementary to a wife, husband or child. However, their answer has nothing whatsoever to do with what you just told them or quizzed them about! This may be one of many reasons why frustrated family members repeatedly talk instead to pet dogs, cats and parrots!

Pets do not tend to back talk or argue. Sure they bark, meow, chirp, bellow and make all sorts of sounds appropriate to their species. They can and do communicate for themselves, and indeed, once in a while, their nature-conscious owners do actually listen.

There is no denying, however, the incredible enchantment generated among humans and pets. A movie reflecting this love and inducing animal lovers' tears is Hachi: A Dog's Tale. It is based on a real story about a Japanese Akita dog so true to its master that it continued to frequent its guru's haunts for years after the man died. The prime one was a people-infested habitat, a local railroad station, where Hachi had regularly met his patriarch after he arrived there on his way home from work. After the master's death, it became Hachi's home grounds.

Constantly the handsome blond long haired dog sat on the station's steps looking out expectantly to await a master who never arrived. Station users and neighbors adopted him and fed him. They knew Hachi could never be taken home, because he would always insist upon returning to the railway station to wait endlessly near the spot where his master arrived most evenings after work. (Footnote one)

But, even more amazing than these habitual interactions among pets and their keepers, are the surprise spirited communications among wild creatures and the environmentally sensitive people of all ages.

A sweet inspiring story inside the Iranian movie, The Color of Paradise, may be fiction, but is so dramatic and heart-felt, it has to have its roots in reality. Eight year-old Mohammad (Actor Mohsen Ramezani) is waiting for his father to pick him up for summer vacation at the institute for the blind in Tehran.

As usual, this intense bird listener begins paying close attention to the cries of a baby feathered one in distress. It fell from its nest and was threatened with murder by a roaming house cat. So Mohammad got down on his hands and knees to hear better. He crawled along ground looking for the baby. As the youngster did so, he heard the cat stalking around the bushes, picked up some stones, twice throwing them in the general direction of that predator's sounds, scaring the clawed, furry one away.

Mohammad finally found the diminutive feathered one by carefully feeling his way along the ground with his fingers. Then, he carefully put the struggling bird in his breast shirt pocket. All the while, Mohammad heard repetitious bird screeches above him in a small tree.

Courageously, the small boy pinpointed that tree and awkwardly after several attempts, climbed it. He felt his way along a branch eventually putting his fingers into a nest where still another baby bird loudly chirped. That little one pecked at Mohammad's stretched out index finger. Undaunted, the boy used that same finger to pet the baby's head. He then carefully placed the other feathered creature back with its sibling, and with great effort slowly scrambled back to the ground. (Footnote two)

Convincing and impressive confirmation that animals or birds and humans communicate spiritually has been discovered regularly for decades within the human prison population.

Beyond what one might expect, however, the wild or tame four-legged or winged ones turn out to be the critical, positive and controlling influences. Chickens, pigeons, ducks, horses and dogs tame murderers, sex offenders, drug dealers, and even the legally insane.

For example, in the 1970s mentally disturbed inmates at the Oakwood Forensic Center in Lima, Ohio, secretly befriended a wounded sparrow. They fed it insects and nursed it back to health in an institution broom closet, writes Earl O. Strimple in his "History of Prison Inmate-Animal Interaction Programs."

After David Lee, a psychiatric social worker, discovered how well the sparrow was influencing its inmate caretakers, he started a year-long study, comparing inmates living with and without pets. "The ward with pets required half the amount of medication, had reduced violence...and no suicide attempts...while the (pet-less) ward had eight suicide attempts," Lee concluded.

Since the early 1900s, it has not been at all unusual for corrections officials to utilize animals and birds to rehabilitate career criminals. Struggling, depressed humans behind bars developed calm and happy personalities not long after geese, other birds, dogs, or other animals became their constant companions.

The inmates' cohabitations with dogs became double successes. Prisoners trained canines for helpful missions outside of prison. One of many such programs, "Puppies Behind Bars," based in New York City, creates guide dogs for the blind after inmates trained the canines inside two state prisons.

On the other hand, the dogs too could be considered 'calm, cool and collected' trainers for their inmate handlers. As they train the dogs, inmates' personalities dramatically change from angry and nervous to friendly and calm. Homo sapiens' interactions or communications with the spirits of wild animals, birds and fish is not nearly as common as they are with dogs, cats and other common pets. Nevertheless, that astonishing mental telepathy exists constantly within nature's wild, awe-inspiring spiritual and indigenous atmosphere.

Humans, with their almost total concentration upon one another and the horrendous environmental and societal problems they create, do not pay enough attention to the beauties of nature they observe day after day.

Nature's Images: So Sweet Dreamlike, So Spiritual! Check out the sunset off the island of Bermuda's coastline.

Bermudian sunsets are among the most dramatic anywhere! Red, orange, blue light sears the ocean's waters! (Photo by Dennie Williams)

Envision the rainbow colors of flowers, the majestic blooming trees, the wandering bears, the buzzing bees, the swooping swallows or sea gulls, as well as the sun-filled country sightseeing near gurgling brooks, lapping lakes, or wave-crashing oceans.

Think of the sun rising over the wandering dark blue rivers inside immense valleys worldwide. Or, contemplate a walk through deep woods near a flowing brook or stream; or a saunter into a huge, lush, waist-high grassy field at midnight under a full orange-yellow moon; and then another walk the next day in the rising multicolored sunlight of an early morning.

Oh Great Night Spirits! Hear that aforementioned water gushing over a stream's large rocks amidst row upon row of nearby trees. Then, move stream side to a pool, look down and gaze at a quivering moon image reflecting in the blue-black rushing waters. Afterward, look up skyward and view the actual half moon face: vague outlines of round creases for eyes, a funny curved line for a nose and a big irregular lined, smiling mouth.

In the fall, when the multicolored leaves are falling, observe the Shepaug River in Washington, Connecticut, from the very middle of its cabled wooden bridge. As the eyes trace upstream, the scene is glorious. A multitude of trunks and branches of varying sized trees on the riverbank reflect into the light brown stream of water moving toward and under you.

It's mid-afternoon with one of the brightest fall suns radiating piercing bright yellow rays. Inside the water, all of the colors create a lengthy, gigantic impressionist work of art. The robin's egg blue sky dominates the stream's center on most sunny, clear days, but can be overtaken as one walks in other bridge directions or times by orange sunlight mixed with dominating fall green, yellow, orange and brown leaves.

Look up from the river to the hills above to see a few dominating pines towering over the wider oaks and maples down below nearer the river. Walk away from the bridge along the river on a path on one side or a dirt road on the other. The river becomes dazzling white in the sun as it curves around the corners over the rocks or reflects either light or dark sky blue as one looks at a wide angle upstream.

A change of scene and time! A spring morning arrives in a Litchfield, Connecticut woodlands near a big farm field. The awakening is the sound of the wind blowing through multi-pointed Maple leaves. First the sound is a soft, rushing one, like water flowing swiftly through a narrow brook. But, as the wind increases, it becomes more like a rock-covered waterfall. It slows and the sound drops to gentle again. In the foreground, light green leaves wave back and forth on their stems.

Deeper and higher in the air, they and their branches create scores of ghostly shadows against the light blue sky and the sparkling bright yellow light of the sun. A solo male red Cardinal sings lightly, and then a Robin joins in. Seconds later, the Cardinal and its pink-brown mate sing in tandem. Other birds chirp and sing farther away. Some of these birds flew thousands of miles, round trip from more southern climes to return to New England in the spring to sing the songs nature's fans have come to enjoy and know so well. Some even fly thousands of miles one-way without stopping much.

Still another awe-inspiring scene! Walking along the banks of a famous steep, far western canyon in a spring, summer, fall or winter day, first see a morning orange-pink sun peaking and tinting in the panorama among the fluffy grey-blue cumulus clouds. As the day wares on through constant hiking up and down and down and up steep inclines, the sunset approaches. Stop again along the canyon wall and wait a minute or two to see the fading sun gradually disappear into the horizon. The elongated puffy clouds are now a deeper shade of orange as the darkness lurks and the water below rushes by. Scenes like sunrises or sunsets inside river canyons become spellbinding or hypnotic for humans, birds, animals and insects alike.

Discover glory contained inside Arizona's Grand Canyon! There one tall, sunburned, elderly, tan, cowboy-hated, federal ranger guide once told my wife and I and a group of other tourists a short bit of fascinating history. It is one mile from the canyon's top to the Colorado River's surface below, he explained. It took one million years for the river to dig down 50 feet of that 5,280-foot distance, he continued. What a dredge! Although geologists say the limestone rims of the canyon formed 270 million years ago, they insist the canyon carving occurred five to six million years ago. (Footnote three)

Those canyon visions never leave memories of the appreciative. Of course, some just don't get it! I heard one woman backing away from the edge of the canyon seriously exclaiming: "It just looks like a great big hole to me!" On the other hand, my first impressions simultaneously made me short of breath and filled with nature-image hallucinations. I slowly backed away from the edge. Awe was within me, not fear. Only one other time have I ever felt so breathless. That was the moment I watched my son, Tommie, being born inside a hospital delivery room.

Inside the canyon, and elsewhere in this continent, American Indians, sometimes wearing animal skins and bird feathers, recognized and practiced natural energy talk. They interpreted wild critters' communications while regularly listening closely to them and watching their movements eons before those from other regions arrived on the shores of Plymouth Rock or islands near South America.

Indians appreciate wild creatures as equal spiritual beings. When they hunt, they ask spiritual permission. They use their quarry to eat or produce fur. That is part of their belief in the Great Spirit who created the world and lived eternally everywhere. But those arriving in the New World from European, Middle Eastern and African countries, with some notable exceptions, did not seem to have the instincts to interact or communicate with wild creatures.

Even though many arrived with strong spiritual beliefs, they learned much more about the spirituality of nature and the wild when they listened to Native Americans. Unfortunately, though, these immigrants simply took over the country, banished Indian tribes to reservations and generally paid little heed to thoughtful and kind spiritual interaction with critters living on the land, in the air and under the water.

An extreme exception to human attitudes toward wild creatures comes from Buddhists and separately Shamanism, said to be the oldest spiritual tradition on earth.

In her article, "Buddhism and Animals," writer Sharon Callahan, writing in Anaflora.com, says:

"Buddhism considers all of life to be evolving toward higher consciousness. To the Buddhist, any practice by which man sustains himself at the expense of other sentient beings is considered wrong. Buddhism considers non-human life to be Divine just as is human life. Animals are seen to be an evolving kingdom of living creatures destined in time to attain perfect enlightenment. All of life is seen to be one. According to this conviction, to harm any living thing is to do injury to the One Eternal and Divine Life. Since animals are considered to be travelling towards enlightenment just as man is, neither are they to be harmed, discouraged or hampered in their progress."

Separately, there is Shamanism.

"In the worldview of the shaman, all life forms are interconnected and interdependent. If one species suffers, all others are affected. The health and wellbeing of humanity is, therefore, dependent upon the overall health of the web of life. The shaman is sensitive to this sacred interrelationship and serves as an intermediary between nature and the community. The shaman's prayerful communion with the natural elements and powers preserves an orderly, harmonious universe. The shaman seeks harmony with nature and the drum serves as an instrument of atonement," says the Shamanic Paradigm. (Footnote four)

On the other hand, some American Indians believe there would be little or no life for man at all without nature's animals, birds, fish and other wild critters. "In the beginning of all things, wisdom and knowledge were with the animals, for Tirawa, the One Above, did not speak directly to man. He sent certain animals to tell men that he showed himself through the beast and that from them, and from the stars and the sun and moon should man learn all things tell of Tirawa," said Eagle Chief (Letakos-Lesa) Pawnee.

"What is man without the beasts? If all the beasts were gone, man would die from a great loneliness of the spirit. For whatever happens to the beasts, soon happens to man. All things are connected," said Chief Seattle, chief of the Suquamis (Footnote five) "…animals do not 'smell' human emotions, but instead possess a form of ancient mental telepathy or method of thought transference not understood by modern man. Animals do communicate with man by receiving mental messages and they carry this ability with them in spirit as they die," says TAKATOKA. (Footnote six)

"According to Mayan beliefs," says www.animalspirits.com/index1.html , "the journey of the sun across the sky and the darkness of night stood for the eternal journey of human consciousness and its transformations," says animalspirits.com. "The sun at midday was compared to the Eagle, flying high in the sky. Then it plunges below the horizon, just as we plunge into the dark where we face our spiritual challenges and are transformed. The hidden sun was said to be Jaguar, whose spotted skin symbolized the stars glittering in the night sky. Thus, it was called the 'Jaguar Sun.' Jaguar is the earth father. As earth father, he presides over the sacred power in the earth and the animals that live upon it. The force that lives within the mountains, which gives them their volcanic and transformative power, is the same underworld source of power and energy as the Jaguar Sun."

Spirits of birds, animals, reptiles and fish in the wild have their own distinct means of emitting smells or creating vibrating sounds or distinct body motions communicating one to the other. Their diverse messages do not necessarily exclude human beings, even while most humans are oblivious. Usually, people have no idea wild creatures have such cunning, and if you said they did, most look at you as crazed. I know! It happened to me more recently in my later years, when I finally came to understand wild beings!

Expressions or interactions of animals, bird, fish, lizards, snakes and others of the forests, jungles, streams and oceans emerge from sounds, touch, movement as well as smells created by spirits and emotions within them. And, nature's wild creatures are much more tuned in to natural disasters than people are.

Mary Mott writes in Natural Geographic News that:

"Before giant waves slammed into Sri Lanka and India coastlines ten days ago (December 2004), wild and domestic animals seemed to know what was about to happen and fled to safety. According to eyewitness accounts, the following events happened:

- Elephants screamed and ran for higher ground.
- Dogs refused to go outdoors.
- Flamingos abandoned their low-lying breeding areas.

- Zoo animals rushed into their shelters and could not be enticed to come back out."

Biologist and author Rupert Sheldrake, who has written extensively on the intuitive and communicative traits of animals, says: "many millions of pounds are being allocated for setting up tsunami warning systems. I hope that those responsible for spending this money will not ignore what animals can tell us."

It is stupefaction that people do not have the sixth sense bridging them to nature or to impending disasters as wild, instinctive creatures do! What a daily loss for people who fail to have enthusiasm, perception, time, patience or the inner spirit to see, hear, recognize or respect the spirits of other living beings!

Wild critters' spirited, uninhibited expression is beyond and more instinctive than human talk ever is! This becomes repeatedly obvious to many perceptive nature lovers, exploring jungles, deep forests, wetlands, rivers and seas, during the early morning. For them, those natural atmospheric views become so inspirational they begin to conceive that wild critters indeed communicate with humans.

Communication?! Birds sing warble, caw and chant millions of varying tunes or sounds. Frogs croak. Gecko lizards chirp. Cicada-insects vibrate high grate noise. Moneys blare out and cheep. Whales sing repetitiously. Their notes are just as low and high as birds sing. They are a bit like sounds from a cow being milked, but with more varied notes. Dolphins and porpoises bubble off individual underwater clicking and whistling sounds to coordinate activities. (Footnote seven)

Interaction! Dolphins even let humans ride and play with them through the open waters of the ocean. They have extraordinary powers of intelligence. Their interactive or communication skills are beyond man's or woman's conceptions.

The Dolphin Research Center says they can pick up the vocal vibrations of others, including people, through their ample round foreheads. Whistles and clicking noises as well as squeaks and yelps allow them a sophisticated conversation with others for mating, hunting, other fish and socializing. Their social connections include family and males, who bond to one another, and even large groups.

According to various news reports worldwide, dolphins bond closely enough with people that they have saved a drowning teenager by pushing the youngster out of the water to his nearby boat; and, as well, protected swimming lifeguards by surrounding them when sharks roved nearby.

On the other hand, most believe the Great White Shark is a danger to all surface swimming or scuba diving humans venturing below the ocean. However, some naturalists can float so close to the sharks underwater that they can observe those notorious shark teeth and the riveting blue eyes peering just above those dangerous dentures.

Without fearing harm, one underwater fish fanatic, Mike Rutzen, known as "The Sharkman," has been photographed by CBS's 60 Minutes holding on to the notorious upper body fin, as the shark swims. Rutzen does this after the shark and he become somewhat acquainted. That happens when the shark glides closely by several times, and looks Rutzen over with his big eye. Soon afterward, the shark body-bumps him with his nose. Finally, Rutzen grabs a hold of the shark fin as the fish swims by, and takes a short ride! (Footnote eight)

Obviously, these sharks can be dangerous to humans. Jeopardy lurks when sharks are exceedingly hungry, or when they spot sudden movements, creating an alluring target, appearing to be a fish, a seal or a squid.

"After observing the white sharks at Seal Island for eight seasons, and documenting more than 2,500 predatory attacks, we have arrived at quite a different opinion," said R. Aiden Martin and Ann Martin. "Our research demonstrates that White Sharks are intelligent, curious, oddly skittish creatures, whose social interactions and foraging behavior are more complex and sophisticated than anyone had imagined" the Martins explained in writing "Sociable Killers: New Studies of the White Shark."

And although the Great White Shark's prime reputation is for killing, unlike man, it does so to survive. In case you haven't noticed, sharks don't go to war or use their teeth as the equivalent of piercing swords, or are they serial killers.

More recently, in January 2012, 60 Minutes featured two amazing women, one who monitors elephants to record and video their language and related movements, and the other, who spent years communicating and living with chimpanzees.

For two decades, says Wildlife Direct, Andrea Turkalo, has lived in "a small camp at the Dzanga Baï clearing in the midst of a tropical rainforest in the south-west of the Central African Republic. It is a thirty-minute walk from her camp to the clearing." Wildlife Direct quotes Turkalo: "I have walked 33 thousand kilometres along this path."

Meanwhile, she is working with the elephant listening project which records and videos male, female and baby elephants constantly to create a dictionary of their language. One of the videos depicts adult elephants trying to revive a dead baby in the mud by massaging it with their trunks. Once they become aware it is no longer living, they form a line and sidle by the dead baby in apparent sadness.

Another dedicated naturalist, Dr. Jane Goodall, 77, an English woman, has spent most of her life studying animals in the wild with particular interest in chimpanzees. "In her leisure time, she observed native birds and animals, making extensive notes and sketches, and read widely in the literature of zoology and ethnology," says her biography at www.biogrphy.com/people/jane-goodall-9542363

Beginning her intense nature observations in Africa as a 23-year-old, she continued her extraordinary work for two decades. Today, with obvious joy, she occasionally revisits her animal friends as if they are close relatives.

Three years after her initial experiences in Africa, Goodall began her first studies of chimps in Gombe National Park, Tanzania. She discovered eventually that chimp families, whose members she affectionately named individually, are personable, affectionate and can communicate in various ways.

Videos show her regularly playing with, talking to and affectionately kissing her chimp friends. But, she says, chimps, like humans, can infrequently be violent and do seriously batter or kill other chimps who stray out of territory. She, herself, was dangerously beaten by an adult male chimp. The big black lumberer knocked her to the ground with his front paws, and during the struggle, imposed a head injury, which, fortunately, she recovered from. However, that incident did not deter her from her continued activities with chimps.

Nevertheless, such an incident is indeed a warning for any person working in close relationships with wild creatures. Goodall says some chimps become hostile when they believe another creature is invading their territory.

Every wild creature has its own way of communicating with not just their own kind, but with any living critter who will listen. But those wild creatures, as well as humans, who live in the wildest of environs, concentrate upon survival, the aggressive, kill or be killed, kill to eat and survive. That leaves less time for wild creatures and people to learn to become acquainted and more time for aggressive hunting of one another.

On the other hand, those wild critters living closer to human cultures and populations learn by experience, necessity, and habit to better communicate or interact with people. Some wild creatures, particularly those more used to human populations, have more sophisticated sounds and communicative motions than others.

"Certain behaviors in both wild and domestic animals are governed largely by innate (hard-wired) programs; however, experiencing and learning are the most important factors in other behaviors," say Temple Grandin and Mark J. Deesing in Genetics and the Behavior of Domestic Animals.

For instance, in the extreme arctic climates in the South or North Poles, birds, animals and fish almost never see humans. As well, rare human explorers don't see or experience those wild critters like they might in warmer climes. The extremely cold atmosphere heightens wild creatures' and humans' concentration upon survival, or potentially eat or be eaten, kill or be killed. Leisure time for communications hardly exists.

But animal sounds don't vary much, whether they are in the wilderness or closer to human populations. Wolves howl with varying tones, sometimes with incredibly haunting sounds. "Scientists recognize at least ten different categories of sound (e.g., howls, growls, barks, etc.). Each sound communicates a different, context-dependent message," according to The Wolves and Moose of Isle Royale. Apes use body sign language to communicate critical needs among themselves. They use the same body movements to interact with other animals and humans with less success.

"Animals that live in a dense habitat, such as woodlands, transmit information by a form of Morse code achieved by banging their heads against the roof of their tunnel. ("Blind mole rats, for instance, have this capability through head drumming," says Dr. Karen Shanor, a neurophysiologist at Georgetown University, and her colleague Jagmeet Kanwal, a neuroethologist.) "This means of communication is clearly heard by humans," People's Trust explains. (Footnote nine)

These various creatures are hardly alone in creating message pipelines. Male antelopes move their bodies into blocking positions when they want to either warn females about predators nearby, or pretend to do so. The pretending keeps females nearby for momentary sexual encounters, says a New York Times news story by Sindya N. Bhanoo. (Footnote ten)

Humans need concentration, imagination and insight to penetrate and appreciate the mesmerizing atmosphere within nature's habitats. Ego evaporation is essential in appreciating the glorious drama of walking underneath the sky in the open air.

Spiritual vision must encompass not just the eyes, but the ears, the nose, the feel and the extra sensory powers of the mind for observation. Getting to that uncommon state requires extraordinary interest, a positive attitude and an imaginative outlook toward whatever particular beauty in nature you are smelling, observing or contemplating. True focus of a human's spirit upon a fascinating plant, wild creature or wildlife scene can be a mesmerizing experience. Meditation Oasis writes:

"Our being resonates with the sight of a flower, sound of birds, feeling of the breeze. These experiences wake something up inside of us, and help to set our lives into a more natural rhythm. Nature lovers have discovered this secret without ever studying meditation!" (Footnote eleven)

And, guess what?! Animals, birds, fish and other wild critters too are capable of being spiritual. When humans and wild creatures confront one another with positive spiritual vibes, it becomes inspiring for all involved in the face off.

Of all wild creatures, birds, especially, interact in surprisingly friendly ways toward humans feeding them, talking to them or mimicking their songs and sounds. Observe those flying, hopping, swimming and singing creatures meticulously and patiently in the wild. Listen to and watch them as equal spirits of the hinterlands. Sing and whistle to them!

Some animals and birds actually mate for life. Mother Nature Network cites eleven examples including Swans, Albatrosses, Black Vultures, French Angel Fish, Turtle Doves, naturally, and amazingly, Wolves! (Footnote twelve) This means no divorce like is seen in about 50 percent of the human population worldwide.

What hardy joy people-to-wild-creature communication habits eventually spawn! Do it expertly enough, for instance, and some birds will start to trust you by perching nearby and singing. I was pumping gas in a small city one day, when I spotted a group of small sparrows jumping around, in and underneath a round, small pine bush nearby.

For fun, I began imitating their sounds repeatedly. Within seconds, all of the sparrows made their way to the bush top, and began looking all over for the weird sounding broken whistles. Even the cars driving by or the sound of an ambulance's siren didn't stop their ears from listening to the 'wheets, stweets' from that stranger. These birds' ears are on the sides of their head near the bottom outer edge of their eye, says Yahoo Answers.

Ian Gereg is about as close to birds on a daily basis as anyone can be. As Director of Aviculture and Education for The Livingston Ripley Waterfowl Sanctuary in Litchfield, Connecticut, he has had a lifelong interest, particularly in waterfowl. His biography on the sanctuary's Internet site says, "Ian has accrued working experience with over 100 species of ducks, geese, and swans (and) a variety of other groups of birds."

Like other close observers of wildlife, he can sense what birds are thinking. One day, I asked him why a particular male Hawaiian (Ne Ne) goose, whose head constantly moved up and down, kept waddling intensely along a sanctuary fence. The bird, I said, squawked out goose alert noises as people walked by.

When I walked right up to the fence and greeted the goose, I said, he faced me and made a more friendly continuous sound. The goose's mate, Ian replied, had recently died so he was in mourning. His travels had become so regular and brisk, said Ian, that he injured his leg and needed first aid. Unfortunately, medical attention failed so the goose was euphemized. Hopefully, mow he is back with his loving mate in the world above!

These are Ian's descriptions of his own interactions with flying creatures.

"Over the years as birds come and go in my life, several stand out in my mind because of their distinct personalities," he explained. "While most were remarkable in their calm, friendly manner, others remained ingrained in my memory as holy terrors. As one of my mentors once said 'birds are like little people with feathers, they love, mourn, cheat and display lots of other human emotions."

"Early in my avian memories I remember my first experience with killdeer," Ian said, "a common species of plover in Connecticut. Their remarkable broken wing display, feigning injury to lead predators away from their nest and eggs, always intrigued me as I watched them on the schoolyard. As social creatures, waterfowl, the ducks geese and swans are inclined to show attachments to family life. Whether bonded to their genetic parents, a foster caregiver, or even a human, waterfowl strive to maintain bonds with their perceived 'family'. Through working with a variety of species, I've encountered some remarkably sociable birds," Ian said.

"The drive to protect offspring, often involving the potential loss of life or limb to the (protecting) parents, has always impressed me. Whether it's a pair of fist-sized ringed teal angrily threatening in defense a clutch of newly hatched ducklings, or a red-breasted goose, flying kamikaze style into the face of an encroaching human, the parental investment in their young overrides all fears. (It includes) broken wings, shattered fighting off an aggressor, to eventual death at the hands of a raccoon, as a mother sits silently and tenaciously on her nest," Ian observed.

Ian watches the activities of feathered ones closely at the sanctuary all year around. Here is a taste of his November 2010 Avian Update:

"As we humans prepare for winter weather, some of the birds at the Conservancy have other projects to attend to. Our Cereopsis Geese have begun to work on their nest, a process that first starts with the male selecting a nest site, and making a shallow nest site scrape in the ground. Once the initial construction is complete, the male gives way to the female who completes the nest building."

"Along with the Cereopsis, our Hawaiian geese are beginning to show signs of nesting interest. Both of these goose species are the first of our waterfowl to nest each year, with the first goslings usually hatching in January."

"While a few of our birds are preparing to nest, the majority of the waterfowl at LRWC are beginning to acquire their colorful alternate plumage to woo a mate for next spring. It's exciting to see color returning to the aviaries as species, like common mergansers and king eiders, make headway towards attaining their bold winter plumage. Many of our other ducks have already attained their breeding colors, and several photography and nature groups have visited recently to take advantage of the recent flush of color."

So it is impossible or imaginary that birds, animals and fish communicate or interact with humans? Think about this: a totally unknown person approaches, smiles and even starts to jabber as if they have known you for years? Why is this happening?! The stranger senses a friendly spirit, matching his or her own, so the interloper cannot resist smiling and chatting spontaneously. Sometimes just body language connects strangers. On the other hand, birds, animals and fish instinctively and regularly interact with all other living beings inside their natural universe. It's their sounds, body movements, eyes, characteristics and spirits which communicate seemingly better than the languages of human beings.

Even predators, when not hunting quarry, have the absolute need to communicate regularly in friendly ways. On the other hand, their potential prey may accidentally get a life saving warning through that very predator's or another animal's or bird's sounds, movements or smells. When birds and animals are not hunting their victims, friendly communications from those predators emanate routinely. Yet never or hardly at all do such warm sounds emerge from predator humans? People clearly are the earth's most destructive force.

Unlike wild creatures, they kill and despoil randomly, sometimes just for the thrill of it. Some humans' inability to appreciate nature in the slightest regularly leads to tragedies for nature and the environment. It's those supposedly intelligent humans who create industrial oil and chemical spills, as well as, radioactive emissions and polluted air and water. Their carelessness is gradually killing, maiming, sickening or polluting worldwide. They create living hell and care less. Climate change, denied by most of these same polluters, is creating more and more tornadoes, earth quakes, tsunamis, and unusual weather patterns.

Ironically, for instance, some human-spread poisons lodge inside fish that survive only to be caught by fishermen. Then the fishermen or their customers get sick eating them. Yet even then, few, including the fishermen, ever try to trace down the source of the fish poisoning unless it is wide spread.

Only humans continuously pollute air, water and earth with all the chemicals they manufacture to make money, money and more money to feed their ugly human hungers and egos.

The most incredible example lately, in 2010, was the British Petroleum's oil platform explosion in the Gulf of Mexico off Louisiana, killing eleven workers, injuring sixteen. In the meantime, the oil slick sickened and killed untold numbers of birds, fish, turtles and wild life and plants of all kinds exposed to the ugly oil trail.

The discharges extended into the coastlands of five states. It will take decades to measure the devastation spreading west to Louisiana and Texas and east to Mississippi, Alabama and Florida.

Seeing the Pelicans, Sea Gulls, Terns, Herons and Ospreys covered with oil makes nature lovers ill with sadness.

Many people living along the Gulf of Mexico and nationwide are so concerned with the harm to fishermen's and shore dwellers' professions that the monumental toll on wildlife is not much of a focus. It has been, however, for environmentalists who have made heroic efforts to clean up birds and save turtle eggs to relocate them to safe areas far away.

Only humans regularly create such environmental disasters, as well as drawn out, deadly wars among themselves, leaving hundreds of thousands dead and despoiling the earth with fall out from weaponry to kill thousands more, and despoil nature.

Incredibly, while some evil dealers carried out the illegal drug trade; or paramilitary warlords conducted business; or circus managers operated in Colombia, South America, they all captured hosts of wild pets later needing rescuing from those criminals' negligence.

According to a story in The New York Times, Ana Julia Torres, a career animal lifesaver, made many of the injured wild creatures a home and saved their lives. (Footnote thirteen) In a startling Times photo, taken by Meridith Kohut, Torres kisses the drugged and disabled Jupiter The Lion on the lips through the bars of a cage.

Said Joseph Conrad: "The belief in a supernatural source of evil is not necessary; men alone are quite capable of every wickedness." James Anthony Froude opined: "Wild animals never kill for sport. Man is the only one to whom the torture and death of his fellow-creatures is amusing in itself."

However, it is only fair to mention that many humans regularly risk their own lives in sometimes futile attempts to save declining animal and bird populations.

Valmik Thapa, a naturalist of India, spent most of his life protecting Tigers, ravaged by poachers he vows to shoot in self-defense. Poachers, he says, will fire at anyone who attempts to intercept them. In answering 60 Minutes newsman Scott Pelley's 2007 program question about what would happen if all Tigers were murdered, Thapa said: "For me, life will not be worth living...The tiger is the sentinel. The tiger is the great symbol that keeps this quality of the natural world alive. Therefore, people like me will fight for it till the last day I'm alive."

On the other hand, there is no question that if a tiger is hungry, the man-eater will leap on and devour a human like it would any animal. But, unlike a human, a tiger usually kills only what it needs for breakfast, lunch or dinner. Humans slaughter animals, birds and other wild creatures for the fun of it, for money, or just for a pelt or a dead feathered sculpture to show off to anyone.

Again, unlike human kind, animals, birds, fish and reptiles have nature's sense to be satisfied once they have eaten enough. Yet, poachers constantly kill animals for money, while others hunt, fish and spear just for the thrill of it.

"The poachers, and especially those involved in the rings, are thieves... They are not even hunting – they are simply killing," says Larry S. Moore, an Ohio hunter. (Footnote fourteen)

Many hunters throughout history, back to the days of the caveman, hunted to feed themselves and survive, just as some animals, birds and fish do. Some of those critical of hunters or fishermen cannot understand how they can be fond of the wildlife they kill. Yet many of those critics, who call themselves nature lovers, regularly eat the meat of those creatures as well as the cattle and chickens often kept confined in mass inside pens or cages just for their eventual slaughter.

As expressed in "American Indian Philosophy" by Karlton Douglas, many American Indians, although hunters to their core, had an incredible respect for all animals, even and especially those they killed.

Douglas wrote inside www.Melugeons.com: "They held land in common as a tribe, but it was as if they were borrowing it from the Creator, and using it for the tribe's benefit. In the same way hunting animals was in a sense, borrowing animals for their food from both the Creator, and the animal itself. They held animals in high regard generally — seeing them as fellow creatures. As or personal Fetishes, some Indians had a near worshipful attitude toward certain specific animals. Other Indians held that particular animals were their personal guardians, much like Christians consider themselves protected by guardian angels. Again, to the Indian you could no more own the earth than you could the sky, or the ocean. It was on loan to the people to keep in trust for the following generations."

The Handbook of American Indians North of Mexico agrees: "The bear, after having been killed, receives marks of reverence; and the first game animals obtained at the beginning of the hunting season must be treated with particular care. The complicated customs related to buffalo hunting and the salmon ceremonials of the Northwest Indians, as well as the whale ceremonials of the Eskimo may also be given as examples."

As one of those stargazers who has sung and spoken, especially to birds, almost all seven decades of my country living, I, like the American Indians, believe their spirits, songs and movements enlighten and rejoice human spirits. They do not have to be singing at, flying towards, or focusing on me or anyone else directly to do that. Pay close attention to them always! Eventually, the beauty of their sounds, their bodies and souls, their energy, their spunk and their resolve will overcome the soul.

With Close Appreciation Comes Amazing Sights and Spirits.

One day, I was working out at a Litchfield, Connecticut, fitness center on a leg muscle machine. My lower limbs were moving rapidly from side to side, with weights in place, and they reflected my action in the huge, floor to ceiling, picture window two feet in front of me.

Suddenly, three Chickadees flew into a bush. Its tiny bare branches held a few dead leaves, touching the picture window. The birds sported black caps, startling dark oval-shaped eyes, tiny grey beaks, black beards, white cheeks, light orange-buff breasts, sharp grey wings and tiny, clawed feet. It was late fall. The morning sun's rays both peeked and fired through the clouds in streaks of various widths.

Three little flighty ones, just about the diameter, when flapping, of a musical CD disk, sang, danced, hopped and flew a few inches from branch to branch. Suddenly, one of the birds flew onto the window trying to attach itself to the glass. Its little clawed-feet slid down the pane with wings flailing, before it backed away, and flew back to the nearby branch.

Within seconds, a second Chickadee hopped from another branch, attached its claws to the frame of the same window, and pretended to peck at an invisible seed. "No nourishment there," I thought with amusement. Back it flew to the bush to again hop from branch to branch with its two hopping buddies. Within 30 seconds of their theatrical performance, they simultaneously flew off across the parking lot, and disappeared into the trees.

Astonished, I called out spontaneously to three young women gabbing and stretching nearby. I loudly recreated that bird performance as best I could. I concluded with a mock chicadee-dee-dee chirp. Laughs followed, but then I hesitated to tell them the Chickadees were showing off! They might have thought I was nuts!

That is not the only time such a bird show has happened. During the spring, I was talking in the woods with my son, Tommie, and with a wildlife expert on the scores of invasive species strangling the trees nearby. The invasives had sent their winding vines into bushes and trees everywhere as we looked deep into the downhill section of the forest. One vine was ingrained into and strangling a tree stem and its bark.

The three of us were up on one of the most beautiful hills, overlooking much of the historic Town of Litchfield. The sky was mostly cloud cover, but the sun pierced brightly through the cracks in the huge moving, fluffy ones. As our conversation progressed, I noticed a small, cute, normally people-shy Yellow Warbler chirping on a branch only a few feet above us. Its light yellow body contained light brown lines. Its wings had a grey tint. Its tiny dark grey beak and round dark marble shaped eyes made it irresistible to its mates or to appreciative human eyes.

Three male voices reverberated through the tree branches. The Warbler chatted along with us, and hopped from branch to branch as if he was looking for a place to nest. "See-see-see-titi-see," and just, "titi-see, titi-see," the Warbler called repeatedly right at us. It continued chatting and hopping almost until we walked away, between five and ten minutes' later. The little fellow disappeared without a trace, not even a single Titi-see.

So what was the warbler doing? He seemingly wanted in on our energy and conversations about the surrounding forest. Even if he didn't, he miraculously created that impression.

If you don't believe birds communicate with humans, then you need to see it on film inside the YouTube site on the Internet. One of the best nature videos I have seen on that site reveals how the Maasai tribe in East Africa discovers their treed honey comb by whistling with "the Honey Guide bird." The tribe members start conversations with those winged creatures through their whistles. The Honey Guide answers with a unique call it uses to show them the way to the honey. Tribe members follow the bird's calls from tree to tree.

Tribesmen know they are getting close when the beautiful big grey breasted bird with a light blue back cries out a special alert. Wow! There's the tree with the buzzing bees inside a hollow wooden chamber above.

Using smoke from a small lighted tree limb pointed down into the chamber to slow and confuse the bees, the tribesmen dig the honey out, while getting stung several times, despite the smoke. Before leaving, the honey gatherers left part of the honey comb with added grubs inside it on the ground nearby as the Honey Guide's reward.

Sure enough, as the honey hunters depart the scene, the happy bird drops down and pecks away at the grubs inside the broken honey comb. The BBC film announcer jokes that if the tribesmen didn't leave their reward, next time, the honey bird would probably lead them to a lion's den instead. (Footnote fifteen)

Oh, OK, I'm harking back to how the warbler that my son, myself and the environmentalist observed in the woods that day, and its reaction to us! Well, the experienced bird sanctuary manager I know, Mr. Gereg was showing me the nature preserve and duck ponds near our home one day. As he explained the ponds and bird life around us, a group of a half dozen baby white geese followed at his heels. When Ian spoke, they made regular, loud clucking sounds. When he fell silent and stopped walking, they did too. I looked directly at him and exclaimed: "What are these baby geese doing?!" Ian immediately replied, "They think I'm their mother." That is logical, since Ian has cared for those geese ever since they broke out of their eggs.

A friend of mine, Jay Abbott, a hunter and nature lover too, says he once was intent upon hatching quail eggs, but had to leave home and get in his car for a long trip. But, he couldn't bear to leave the ready to hatch eggs at home. One quail, the size of a large Bumble Bee, had already hatched, so that chick became a passenger.

Inside his car on the front passenger seat across from one of the vehicle's heating ducts, Jay readied for further imminent births. He created a plastic bubble to house the eggs' birthing box. After he drove away from home and was on the road for twenty minutes, says Jay, he heard a resounding "Peep Peep Peep!" He stopped the car to look over into the plastic bubble. The quail baby had turned to look at him, and noisily alert him to the birth of two siblings, just breaking their eggs.

Jay says he stopped for a brief celebration with the chicks, before driving on. Time wore on. Another outburst of peeping ensued within another twenty-five miles of driving, says Jay. By then, he explains, the chicks believed the car's inside had become unbearably hot. So he turned down the heat, opened the window and put his head outside as he drove on, he says. But the little quails were still protected from the window's air rush inside the warm plastic bubble.

Within 25 miles more of driving, says Jay, he heard another emphatic "Peep Peep Peep." He looked over to see one or more of the baby quails looking at him expectantly. "Oh," he thought, "it's getting too cold for them." So he turned up the heat. Sometime later when the temperature became too hot, says Jay, they all began peeping loudly until he turned down the heat again. When the comfortable temperature returned, he says, they fell mostly silent. The sequence kept repeating itself, Jay explains, until hours later when he finally ended the road trip inside Cape Cod. "Upon reflection," Jay says, "I felt quite privileged to have been in such a direct and unmistakable communication with such young and tiny members of our animal kingdom."

A dramatic quote from Beyond Human Communication by Harvey 'Walks with Hawks' Doyle makes the point: "I have observed the Red Tail Hawk for years and they have their way of communicating with others. You must study and watch them and study them. They are good communicators. You must be alert to positive and negative energies and also their movement in the air and when they are resting. When you learn more of energies, and that Mother Earth is alive; then you will begin to understand the language of her inhabitants. We should realize to be a part of the circle of life we must know how to communicate."

Now, nationwide, colleges and universities are awakening their students to interaction and intercommunication among wild creatures and humans. It's an exciting development. More young people will become aware of the need to protect birds, animals, fish, all creatures and the environment. That is critical to the future of the health of the world. (Footnote sixteen)

Footnote one: Sony Pictures Movie directed by Lasse Hallstrom. Hachiko is also the subject of a 2004 children's book named Hachiko: The True Story of a Loyal Dog, written by Pamela S. Turner and illustrated by Yan Nascimbene. American movie starring actor Richard Gare, directed by Lasse Hallstrom http://www.nidokidos.org/threads/44498-A-dog-waited-his-owner-Nine-Years-(True-Story-)

Footnote two: The Color of Paradise, a Sony Pictures Classic, written and directed by Majid Majidi

Footnote three: http://www.ohranger.com/grand-canyon/grand-canyon-geology

Footnote four: http://shamanicdrumming.com/shamanic_paradigm.html

Footnote five: Both Indian quotes from Native 'American
Indians Quotes and Thoughts
http://www.stevenredhead.com/Native/
Footnote six: Source

http://www.manataka.org/page291.html#TALK%2
0TO%20THE%20ANIMALS

Footnote seven: From People's Trust for The Environment and EverythingDolphins.com.

Footnote eight: CBS 60 Minutes
http://www.cbsnews.com/stories/2010/03/25/60minut
es/

Footnote nine: People's Trust for the Environment.

Footnote ten: New York Times article
http://www.nytimes.com/2010/05/25/science/25o
bantelope.html?ref=science

Footnote eleven: Meditation Oasis
http://www.meditationoasis.com/how-to-
meditate/simplemeditations/nature-meditations/

Footnote twelve: http://www.mnn.com/earthmatters/
animals/photos/11-animals-that-mate-for-life/

Footnote thirteen: New York Times article at
http://www.nytimes.com/2010/03/31/world/americas
/31colombia.html

Footnote fourteen: Buckeye Firearms Association by Larry S. **Moore**
http://www.buckeyefirearms.org/node/3986

Footnote fifteen: YouTube
http://www.youtube.com/watch?v=N6jVvZrxpUs

Footnote sixteen: New York Times article
http://www.nytimes.com/2012/01/03/science/animal-studiesmove-from-the-lab-to-the-lecture-hall.html?pagewanted=all

Now, after seven decades of life, the man and this book's author, who feeds the Chickadees, is an old dude. But, as my father always said: "Age is just an attitude, and I don't have one!" As humans we need to patiently stand by while watching and listening carefully to the creatures of nature communicating to us. This poem about Chickadees, one of my favorite sprightly, energetic little birds reflects the spirit of that interaction.

Chickadees and The Ancient Birder

Floating down, floating down from blue cloudy sky came white fluffy snowflakes,

Like tiny frozen irregular shaped puzzle pieces originating from frozen white clouds above.

They drifted in slow motion out of huge white and grey clouds through dusty grey-blue skies.

The sagging limbs of five-foot bushy Hemlocks nearby accumulated that white frozen fleece, turning their green bough tops ashen.

And there, fast free air winging, then veering into those green snow covered sprigs was the tiny Black-Capped Chickadee:

White breast and cheeks like the snow fluff;

Jet-black head cap and matching triangular mustache beneath itty-bitty black beak;

Light orange feather semi-circle throat underneath sharp grey wings;

And bitsy, dark grey legs and feet claws.

It abruptly hop-bounced from one snowy twig to the next.

Couldn't stay still!

Even when perched, it quick-moved side-to-side readying for the next short jump-flight.

Suddenly, two companions flew into separate boughs

Above and below the first.

Immediately more chirping began – seemingly one to the other:

Two-note whistles, fee-bee fee-bee,

Followed rapidly with the signature refrain, Chicka-deedee Chicka-deedee Chicka-deedee!

A grey, rumple-haired old man, short black-coated in blue overalls and black boots walked onto the scene.

Holding a round, orange plastic funnelled birdseed container, He headed to a small plastic-tubed bird feeder. Chickadee communications intensified.

Those sounds seemed to harmonize with every snow crunching boot step.

And, as the man began filling the feeder, one of the excited feathered creatures, flew out from a pine bough to two-foot naked bush just feet away.

Meanwhile, the other two mates hopped closer to the very end of the green-white boughs.

All three were now alternately chipping and belting out notes de-de-de- or Namesake chants: Feebe-Feebe or Chicka-deedee Chicka-deedee Chicka-deedee!

Those are signals one to the other, coordinating their next moves, or sometimes sounding alarms!

The nearest by bushed bird blew out,

Inches over the slowly backpedalling man's right shoulder;

Before landing on the feeder; looking from side to side;

Pecking out a sunflower seed;

Veering his feather cluster away; and winging air into the Hemlocks.

As the staring, smiling man stood still, a couple of feet from the feeder, two others followed their mate's example, flying boughs to feeder for a couple of seed pecks, and back, within seconds, into the Hemlocks.

All three then simultaneously flew off again into a nearby huge Maple,

But not too far! They perched on a couple of leaf-bare twig-branches, then cried again and again:

Chicka-deedee Chicka-deedee Chicka-deedee!

That's exactly what those birds called: communication promoting instant results!

Despite being deeply appreciative of wildlife as a small boy, it wasn't until I lived all of seven decades that I had a startling experience making me realize there exists an inspiring spirit connecting all living beings.

The first short story that follows recounts two related experiences persuading me to write all the rest of the tales. It convinced me beyond all doubt that all living beings can communicate or interact, even if most do not exercise those talents. Sometimes the interaction seems like a vivid, beautiful dream, bringing human and mammal or bird or fish into an inspiring spiritual universe together. On other occasions, however, humans become startled by hostile wild life reactions to their own unfriendly or thoughtless activities: reactions, it seems, they full well deserve.

Blueberries, Butterflies and The Pig

Picking blueberries one after the other under cloudy, but still sunny skies in a big netted over blueberry patch on a beautiful hill in little ole New Preston, Connecticut!

Clumsy hands induce little blue, green and red ones to fall to the earth and roll below. Some others are already mashed into the soil. Big chubby ones go down the hatch. Sometimes red, orange and green ones drop accidentally into blueberry containers.

Chatter comes from a couple of bushes nearby. Two elderly ladies are bantering back and forth about their ailments; their hubbies' doctor visits; hospital care for everyone; and all available medical treatments. The babble becomes annoying fast!

Picking, picking, picking more blueberries! I'm not fast enough! Already Ina, the Mom and my wife, has filled her plastic gallon drinking water bottle with the top cut open. Mine is not even half full! As usual, she calls for my container to check it and me out. I pretend not to hear her, and shamefully rush my fingers into picking more berries!

Soon, Ina moves over and takes control of my container, leaving me to pick from one hand into the other before walking repeatedly nearby to dump the full hand into the bucket.

The picking goes on and on! Will it ever stop? Oh yes, the buckets both are almost full now, and picking under the sun makes me sweat! For a second or two, my right arm, ready to pick, extended straight out in front of me.

Suddenly a little orange butterfly with miniature black specks flies speedily around me and lands right on the back of my extended right hand! As it retracts its wings, I see the buff orange- brown color on the bottom of those wings, and its two little antlers above its tiny head, and its legs attached to its diminutive body. I glance at the little guy. My outstretched arm and hand freeze. In seconds, the tiny one takes off and flies up and around and then down again on the back of my waiting and frozen right hand. This time it stays.

Here is Dennie next to the very spot where the butterfly landed on his hand in the blueberry patch, but now shown at a later date with a similar butterfly superimposed on his hand in the photo to match what happened. (Photo by Ina Williams & superimposing of butterfly by Tommie Williams)

I wait and wait! I marvel at this little orange-black spotted beauty. Nothing happens! So, keeping my hand and arm outstretched in front of me, I walk slowly, carefully along a couple of blueberry bushes. I show off my new, flying friend-pet first to Ina, who tells me I am just trying to avoid more berry picking. I ignore her and move on to another blueberry picking woman nearby who exclaims surprise, but little else. These relatively unenthusiastic reactions are not at all satisfying! I walk out 75 yards of the blueberry patch while continually looking at my extended right hand, the butterfly's merger airport pad.

The butterfly briefly, during my blueberry bush-to-bush travel, has folded both wings tightly together pointing skyward. Those two wings closed upward become a two-sided pale brown-orange triangle.

As I approach the blueberry patch's wooden payment shack, I see a diminutive little brown-haired boy rolling down a small slope in the grass toward me. A younger pint-sized girl is standing nearby. The boy is laughing and having fun as more grass and dirt cling to his short brown hair, his white t-shirt and his medium blue shorts.

I say firmly to both kids, but quietly: "Hey, want to see my butterfly?!" They look puzzled! I repeat the question. My right arm and hand, holding the sitting butterfly is pointing toward the boy. I exclaim: "Don't move fast!" He looks at it curiously, and of course, moves closer to me. Then, as I move my whole hand slowly upward to keep him from scaring the winged one, the butterfly flits off my hand's posterior.

I look upward. I can see it flying back and forth. It is about twenty feet above me. Seconds pass! I then exclaim: "Hey! Look what you did! It's gone!" Seemingly within seconds, I hear Ina's voice exclaiming a bit sarcastically as she walks out of the blueberry patch: "It landed on your ear!" I immediately replied: "Ha! Ha! You're soooo funny!"

But the little boy quickly cries out, "No it's there on your ear!" My eyes tried to veer a look up there, but naturally, I could not view it. However, I felt a very slight sensation between my right ear and my hair. "Wow!" I thought. "They're right!"

So, I walked slowly and carefully up to the blueberry payment shack. A middle-aged woman was waiting there to weigh blueberry containers and assess cost. Below her lying on the ground were two panting, medium sized dogs, one a blond Husky and the other a black and white long-legged mixed breed. Proudly, I tipped the right side of my head very carefully toward the cashier and asked: "How do you like my butterfly?!"

The woman looked, smiled and seemed amazed. However, as the Husky got up from the ground to greet me with tail wagging and red tongue sticking out of his mouth, off flew the butterfly away into the sky forever! I looked at it disappear. A bit saddened, I petted the Husky and his nearby buddy while Ina, ever the banker, paid for the blueberries.

I thought about this wonderful blueberry patch butterfly mate for several days before an amazing thought suddenly occurred to me. Once before, about ten years back, I had encountered similarly amazing butterfly interactions with another man.

"Whoa!" I exclaimed whispering to myself, after relating the two experiences in my mind. "Butterflies can and do communicate and interact with people, if humans have enough sensitivity to figure this out!"

Now I will tell you that this close to a decade-old story is still relatively fresh in my mind. But, you know that as the years pass, some details can become hazy or exaggerated. Nevertheless, the true guts of this startling story are still etched in my mind today.

That earlier dream-like happening occurred, when, by chance, I met a locally well-known Vermont character, an old, white-haired man, inside the diminutive town of Barnard, Vermont. We both were lingering under the awning of the General Store and looking out onto beautiful Silver Lake nearby.

There were a few part-time porch and pavement below frequenters near us. They included some old guys, young dudes and pet dogs of all sorts, jumping on and off the porch and occasionally into and out of the lake. Across the street, swimmers were just getting out of the lake's cold blue waters onto the green grass alongside. Others were still paddling their arms and hands and splashing inside the nearby shallow portion of a swim hole.

This old white-haired character had been repeatedly seen for years walking up and down the main drag of a road leading south to beautiful Woodstock and north towards diminutive Bethel. He habitually and repeatedly smiled and waved at passing cars, including mine, without hesitation. I later learned his old ramshackle house was just off the main road a mile or two north of the general store which is defined as the town center.

Local residents told me the old man's home had burned to the ground years back, only to be rebuilt by a kindly crew of volunteer townspeople.

So, without warning or hesitation on this very sunny day, the white-haired, winkled-face character sidled right up to my side on that porch, just feet away, and, without introducing himself, began telling his story in a raspy, but riveting voice.

The other night, the dude said, he and a couple of other guys loaded a well used pickup truck with a big, white, muddied pig. He began describing the wild and crazy time they had inducing and pushing the pig up a plank to the bed of the pickup. As he did so with his arms gesticulating in all directions, two medium-sized white butterflies began flying several feet above his head on the edge of the porch and underneath the slanted roof of the General Store!

I don't know whether he saw the butterflies or not, but he never once hesitated in his story telling. In fact, as his story progressed, his arms moved around zigzagging like butterfly wings.

The pig was eventually loaded, he said, before he and another guy got in the truck and drove off, I think, to a pig barn. I wasn't absolutely sure of the truck's destination, because his chattered story became speedier and speedier as it progressed. As the words flew out of his mouth, and he became more excited, the butterflies' flights became faster and more erratic!

Down the road into a wooded area drove the two men with the pig, scrambling and squealing inside the truck's bed. But, because the porker, partially restrained by rope, became wildly squeamish, they stopped and jumped out in a rush to see what the fuss was all about.

It was fortunate, because the hog by now had wriggled out of its moorings and was ready to rock and roll! As the uncombed, white-haired, eccentric, but loveable dude told his story, his long, unbarbered hair flowed from side to side.

Meanwhile, above him the butterflies continued their incredible dance. Up, up, up in the sky they went, only to rush back down to the porch, duck under the roof and then lurch over the old guy's head to match their movements with the gravelly tale teller's voice inflections. Sometimes movements became so dramatic, it was hard to distinguish the flowing white hair from the flying white wings. I was mesmerized!

The two men lost control of the pig as they opened the tailgate to restrain it. It slithered by them, with its body mud flying all over the place, and leaped out of the truck, falling to the ground on its side, and squealing painfully before righting itself and rushing into the woods.

During the yarn, I didn't know whether to watch the butterflies or the old man because both were equally fascinating. I caught glimpses of the butterflies zipping around his head, and once even out a few feet toward the lake before returning, like they were in a magnetic field, to the airways over that wild, messy white hair.

Now, years after hearing the tale, I don't really remember what happened to the pig. I don't think he escaped, but he may have. I do clearly remember this! After the white-haired townsman's lowdown ended, the butterflies simply flew away up into the sky over the lake and disappeared. Amazing! Have you ever seen white butterflies moving around the countryside? They never, ever seem to stop their wild and jagged flight patterns in one location like they did that day!

Butterflies, Flutter-flies Hypnotize

Sunny-warm it is

When butterflies of a myriad of bright colors first
    appear

On the airy, blue sky-lit scene.

Flowers, wild and garden variety, are blooming

Throughout big, flower-filed green fields,

And the well-tended, or chock full of weed gardens.

Scanning out to the buds and the blossoms,

It's impossible not to spot those darting, but silent winged-critters.

They can't avoid the eye! They mesmerize,
    Anesthetize, hypnotize!

Their bright yellow, orange, blue, red or mixed colored wings

Capture the eyes of wild critters, insects and humans alike.

At times, they fly directly over you and air-dance. Other times, they tease and pretend to land, but don't.

Once eyes are close to flowers tended by butterflies, a gaze becomes a rivet on those colorful wings stationery, fluttering or zigzagging the air.

Up, up, up they go, only to dart down, down, down, or maybe up and down or down and up or maybe even, it appears, sideways!

But regularly flower buds of all colors and sizes tempt them.

So, then they instantaneously drop down and land easily, and freeze among the petals with their two dark antennas, as usual, straight up.

They clasp buds with tiny feet at the end of bent wiry legs.

Then, their invisible tongues enjoy a honeyed flower nectar feast.

Sometimes if the flower buds are too deep for the tongue

They drill through a bud leaf to get to the sweets.

If wind, bird, animal, human or even

A nasty predator insect, usually a crab spider or an aggressive bee, scares them upward,

Away they go again, up, up, up, down, down, down,

Or occasionally simply fluttering around!

Sometimes the visits last for seconds, but other stopovers make it seem they, themselves, are bud hypnotized or honey-drugged.

Actually, those longer visits on a plant's leaves can mean butterflies are laying white, bright yellow or even orange round eggs.

Then, they leave one egg nest or flower bud feast to start all over again!

Up, they fly dizzily and down again.

But if the wind gusts blow long and hard enough, butterflies caught in the updrafts, or just beating their wings upward toward the sun, blue skies and puffy white clouds, suddenly disappear.

'Oh, oh, oh!' Think children and nature loving grown ups alike.

'When will we see them again!?'

And the kids imagine:

'Oh boy, if only a beautiful butterfly would land on my hand, my shoulder or my head!'

That's improbable, but not impossible!

As Nathaniel Hawthorne wrote: "happiness is as a butterfly which, when pursued, is always beyond our grasp, but which if you will sit down quietly, may alight upon you."

Butterflies are truly amazing! They, for instance, like birds, bears, penguins and dolphins, know how to connect with humans, even though most humans have a hard time connecting with them. All most of us can do is sense and enjoy their astonishing antics above and around us. But, if anyone believes it's only wild butterflies that might land on a human's hand, think again, because the wildest of birds do it too. Here is such a tale.

Swallow Befriends Sailor As Almost Deadly Sea Storm Drifts Away

For Sailor Christopher Profit a bird in hand is far more inspiring than two in the bush.

His feathered airborne inspiration, a swallow, arrived as his special and sudden sole passenger on the Roberts 27, a twenty-seven-foot long, eight-foot wide sailboat he was steering toward Bermuda. But, mystery is master, so the fascinating details will follow.

The boat he had christened "One Day," while its dinghy life boat, stored in the rear, was nicknamed "At A Time." Christopher purchased "One Day" from a boater in Ithaca, New York, in 1989, and soon trucked it to Rochester, New York. He sailed "One Day" in Lake Ontario for several years before transporting it to Eastport, Maine, where he settled while attending boat building school for two years.

Christopher was twice divorced. His two daughters and a son were adults now, had finished school and were independent. Previously, Christopher held a number of jobs, including as a welder and a silversmith.

One of his most inspiring jobs, lasting eight years, says Christopher, was welding for the famous metal sculptor, Albert Paley. Paley's Internet site says he was: "an active artist for over 40 years at his studio in Rochester, New York, (and) is the first metal sculptor to receive the coveted Institute Honors awarded by the American Institute of Architects."

Christopher's two boats' names came to him from overwhelming appreciation for his rehabilitation through Alcoholics Anonymous. AA's slogan is "One Day At A Time." But, since the back-up dinghy," At A Time," was ripped off "One Day," and drowned during the Bermuda trip storm only "One Day" survives. And, Christopher regularly thanks The Lord for both "One Day's," and his own survival.

Christopher's adventures began off the coast of Eastport, the most Eastern port on the U.S. Atlantic Coast, August 27, 1994. At that time, he was readying to turn 50, and facing "mid-life crisis." Like many sailors of his age, Christopher was restless, and itching for more sea-time. But, more importantly, he was anxious to start a new life. He had been thinking for a while about finding a boat building, boat restoration, or any other employment related to sea traveling apparatuses.

So he decided to sail south down the shores of the Atlantic while job-seeking at various ports along the way. Perhaps, fortunately for Christopher's ultimate fate, he soaked in some tough and adventurous sailing experience, while discovering a couple of safety needs for his Roberts 27 sail boat along the way.

His first challenge was immediate along the huge in-and-out Maine coastline. There even the little waves bounce a small sail boat around in the dark blue water crashing against the bow. Looking toward the rocky shore, waves seem bigger as they burst over the rocks or flip over the beaches, constantly creating alternate loud and soft vibrating sounds. Often, screeching sea gulls follow sails or stray by over head. Bald Eagles occasionally swoon high in the air. Seals bob and weave along the ocean surfaces.

And, if a keen nature seeker is lucky, even an awesome Humpback Whale might surface. On a bright day, sun rays glance off the bobbing waters into a sailor's eyes. As the day turns gradually to night, sunsets can be glorious red, orange, pink or a variety of those colors. But, on a grey cloudy day, there appears to be no horizon, only dark or light grey-blue water melding into similarly colored sky.

As Christopher sailed out of the Eastport canal, the winds and the tides were so powerful he had to use both engine and sails to force the boat out into the ocean. The canal has tides and eddies so powerful some engineers have regularly suggested renewed projects to tap them for energy.

Christopher, nonetheless, made it through the channel safely, after some vigorous sail and tiller work. But, four or five days out, he was stopped and boarded by the Coast Guard off Jonesport, Maine. The Guardsmen soon discovered his small engine did not have the required spark arrestor. The spark arrestor "cools any internal flame or spark created by back-fire, thereby preventing it from igniting fuel vapors inside the engine compartment." (Footnote One)

So Christopher boated into Jonesport Harbor to obtain the required part. He located a Marine store operated by an old Maine salesman-character. After spouting a few words in his classic dialect, the merchant soon made plenty of noisy metal crashing sounds, searching for parts in his rough-hewn boat-part storage shed.

Sailing out of Jonesport, "One Day" then headed for spontaneous visits at a half dozen ports. Christopher mostly focused on job seeking while exploring each seaside town or city. But since no job materialized, he steadily moved south toward Cape Cod, 255 nautical miles from Eastport. (Footnote Two)

After weeks of harbor stops, Christopher finally sailed into Massachusetts' Gloucester Harbor on Cape Ann, a fisherman's and tourist's destination. There the fog became so thick; he sailed around in a maze.

Eventually, Christopher radioed the Coast Guard for a successful one-way fix to discover a safe spot within the harbor. He dropped an anchor the next day to await clearer skies.

A day or so later, Christopher docked for a couple of weeks along Cape Cod's shores at Barnstable. It's the largest community in population and acreage on the Cape, with three canal-like waterways breaking through the beaches in its middle. Agriculture, fishing and salt works are the major industries of this 1600s aged township.

There Christopher visited with his old time friend, John Abbott, an experienced sailor he had known since college days. After shooting the breeze for a while, the two eventually decided to sail together on "One Day" to Martha's Vineyard. Part of the trip entailed a canal voyage, beset with tricky wind and water currents. But, later, they saw nice ocean views slicing by Woods Hole, a charming little town complete with its big Nobsca Point Lighthouse. That beautiful rebuilt structure sticks out on a small bluff with a clear view of Vineyard Sound, a picturesque body of medium blue sea water between Martha's Vineyard and Cape Cod.

Despite his already long, arduous sail, John inspired Christopher to continue on to Bermuda. There Christopher has lived and sailed off-and-on since his teenaged years. His father was a British citizen and became a Bermudian resident when Christopher was six years old. It was not until Christopher was 20-years-old, and decided to attend the school of design at Rochester Institute of Technology, that he moved to upper New York State. But, his brother, Peter Profit, was then still a Bermudian.

Once on shore in Bermuda, John and Christopher theorized Christopher likely could discover the boat building job he sought through sailors, friends and contacts.

They researched and brainstormed the existing weather patterns. The Hurricane Chris, coincidentally nicknamed after "One Day's" captain, had just moved by northward through the Atlantic Ocean. Earlier, late on August 21, Hurricane Chris' slower 40-mile-per-hour winds "passed about 75 miles east of Bermuda. Sustained winds on Bermuda remained below 15 knots. Accelerating north eastward, that hurricane re-strengthened to reach winds of 50 mph.

John's and Christopher's hypothesis was: once Chris had passed northward, it would blow stormy weather away for smooth sailing to the south. Weather.wikia.com says that "by August 24, the deadened storm merged with an extra tropical cyclone southeast of Newfoundland and lost its identity shortly thereafter."

When John left on the ferry back to the Cape, anxious Christopher purchased a GPS, the satellite positioning finder needed for this challenging sail. To be extra cautious, he waited another day before sailing off and heading for the highest point of the legendarily dangerous Bermuda Triangle and Bermuda itself, some 590 nautical miles to the southeast. (Footnote three)

The triangle is "a triangular area...bounded by Bermuda, Puerto Rico, and a point near Melbourne, Florida, in which numerous watercraft and aircraft are said to have mysteriously disappeared," says The Free Dictionary by Farlex. "It happens to be one of the most active shipping areas world-wide."

"The myth of the Triangle started, with the disappearance in peacetime of an entire squadron of 5 US Navy torpedo bombers and their crews while flying a routine training mission off Florida on December 5, 1945," says author Gian J. Quasar in his book, They Flew Into Oblivion. Quasar charges the so called mystery was really breakable: "The Navy's complicity in the disappearance is controversially exposed by liberal use of the original Board of Inquiry proceedings proving they had the evidence to bring back the flight and even to find it after it vanished." (Footnote four)

So the infamous Triangle is usually in a sailor's subconscious while sailing out in the relevant parts of the Atlantic. And, says Christopher, "Going to Bermuda (by sailboat) is like finding a needle in a haystack. (The island) is only 20 miles long and it's a huge ocean!" He estimated the boating trip would take ten days, landing him on the island in early September.

Although Christopher had never sailed to Bermuda, he had the thrill as a 16-year-old to be invited as a crew member aboard a 30 to 35 foot long sail boat that had just finished the famous Newport, Rhode Island to Bermuda race. His mission, among two to three other crew members, he recalls, was to either handle the jib sheet or the main sheet as it sailed from Bermuda to Block Island, part of Rhode Island.

"(Sailing) from Bermuda to the United States is like you are (aiming toward) a big (easy to find) bump," he says. "But sailing the other way (United States to Bermuda) is like a (very) finite destination."

Initially, on Christopher's own initial solo finite trip to the island, everything went smoothly. But, just about 200 miles away from Bermuda, an incredibly dangerous early September tropical depression hit the ocean.

Had he ever been faced with a "Force Ten Gale" like that before while sailing? "No! Never, never in a sailboat! On the ground, I have been through hurricanes in Bermuda. There was one so bad it knocked the plaster from the ceiling down on me while I was sleeping. And, I didn't even wake up! (Instead) I woke up the next morning amidst the rubble!"

Now Christopher was not experiencing gale force winds on land, but instead, those blasting gusts and responding water currents, pushing his small craft repeatedly skyward then ocean-ward; sideways, front ways and backwards. Christopher was awed by "One Day's" amazing buoyancy and durability. "The boat wasn't taking on water. It was just incredible throughout the whole deal. I just knew that I could tough it out and survive."

Here's how he described the first hours of chaos:

"As the storm began to build, I was on deck, with my safety harness clipped onto the boat's safety lines that ran fore and aft with a D-ring right at the companion way."

"First, I took a GPS reading and recorded it on my chart. I then lowered my main and jib sails, and stored them below. I next got every piece of extra rope on board and trailed it off my boat's stern to act as a makeshift sea-anchor, in order to keep my boat's bow heading directly into the waves. "

"I had an (electronic) self steering vane, which a gizmo is attached to the boat's tiller that reacts with the wind so as to keep the boat heading in its set direction. This would allow me to eat or sleep, and (do what I needed to do). But the vane was not much good in gale force winds, so I disconnected it, and lashed the tiller dead center in order to keep the boat pointing into the waves. After making sure that every thing was well lashed down on deck, I went below, closing the hatch securely behind me," he says.

For about two hours after the storm began, Christopher had experienced little time to think of anything else but his mission to baton down the sailboat and its contents, take the sails in and bundle them safely away. One problem eventually developed. The dinghy, "At a Time," was tied and bolted to the rear of the boat. It floated wildly up and down in the turbulence. Ultimately, it filled up with water and was ripped off the boat. It quickly disappeared while sinking into ocean's depths.

The wind-van on the stern of the boat, a big piece of plywood the shape of a sail pointed into the wind. It kept the tiller, preset on the appropriate point with Christopher's supervision. The boat was so small relative to the waves that it acted like a cork. It just went up the waves and down the other sides, a feat a larger boat would not be able to accomplish.

He describes life in the cabin: "Once below deck, I wedged myself on the cabin sole (flooring) in the opening between the salon and fore-peak, which is the area of the boat that moves the least. I then called out to God, and I said, 'If this is my time, I'm ready! I am in your hands!' And I immediately had the feeling that I was literally in His hands, which gave me a great sense of peace!" (Even though, he says, he had never been a particularly religious person.)

"For the duration of the storm, I stayed put there; and really felt like I was in a washing machine! I was really bruised up by being thrown about with every pitch and roll of the boat. For two days, the winds howled and the waves crashed over the boat," Christopher explains.

As time wore on and he was vaguely hungry, Christopher chomped on sardines from a can, as well as some Melba toast. He slept, but only very fitfully. And, amazingly, Christopher says he read quite a few chapters in a thriller novel by Robert Ludlum. His violent and quick-paced action matched the storm, but helped Christopher take a bit of his attention away from those violent winds and waves.

His survival instincts were clairvoyant. After two rocky days, the storm not only cleared, but the weather became smooth for sailing. He describes his surprise:

"Amazingly, the boat's mast was still up and looked just fine. The wind vane was broken. But that seemed to be the only damages from the storm! So I got about putting up sails. The winds were just perfect for being able to set my spinnaker, so I had all my sails up, my main, my jib and my spinnaker....Basically, the weather was broken, the sun was out, the winds were from my stern, and I was on course to Bermuda!...I was just enjoying the movement of the boat, the winds and everything, Christopher explains.

"My left hand was on the tiller...The boat was so steady that once the sails were trimmed, I could almost take my hand off the tiller, and it would stay exactly where it was."

He continues: "And then it happened! The (mostly grey) bird (looking like a cliff swallow) landed on my hand, right on my fingers!"

That left hand was well in front of him resting on and holding the lengthy tiller, extending all the way into the cockpit. That allowed his dorsal mitt to be basically motionless and steady like a piece of sculpture.

"All of a sudden," exclaims Christopher, "(the bird) was there! I didn't see it coming! I only felt it on my hand because I was watching my sails and things...I looked, and there it was. I think I was more amazed than startled by this (seemingly) tiny little thing landing on my hand. I could just feel the tiny little feet. It just looked at me, and I looked at it. And, I just...enjoyed the moment."

"It was just an amazing moment!" says Christopher with noticeable emotion in his voice. "Then, it went to cleaning itself, cleaning all of its feathers...Next it began looking in all directions, but being very aware that I was there. I didn't get any sense of it being afraid or frightened...Then, when its head had rested enough (for what he vaguely estimates was about 15 or 20 minutes), it just flew away," says Christopher.

Time, of course, during an ocean storm in a sailboat, is tough to measure, particularly if a feathered wild critter lands on the unsuspecting sailor. A variety of hungry birds, looking for food, land on boats and rafts, floating in the ocean.

Sea Gulls flap furiously after motored boats with double-deckers, fly up close to the rear and peck food right out of tourists' hands. Usually flocks of starlings and other birds have a better time in a storm, while simultaneously swooping with the winds in circles. But that's generally at a lower wind-speed.

Here's the way some soloists survive hurricane or tropical force winds according to Birding.Com: "Some birds are picked up by the storm system and carried long distances. They become trapped in the calm eye by the towering, fierce storms. The eye of the storm, in effect, becomes a bird cage until the hurricane begins to fizzle and birds can escape. It is the eye of the storm that displaces birds, not the strong winds."

This swallow befriending Christopher, however, was a naturally wild bird that experienced a different wind variety of thrashing, without a hurricane eye. It was probably just fresh from its miraculous survival of the passing storm, and now apparently needed another storm-bashed companion, soon afterward, to calm down its emotions and slow down its fast moving blood stream.

The swallow's presence on his hand, says Christopher, "was an acknowledgment that I had survived, and (the bird) had survived...we had a kind of common bond that we were part of the universe."

Swallows do travel great distances migrating south in the fall across the Atlantic. Some have: "A roundtrip migration distance...as much as 13,600 miles'" says The Migratory Bird Center.

Christopher sailed on without his new found diminutive friend. But, not long after his first visitor, a few beautiful white Bermuda Longtails winged and glided regularly up and around "One Day." He continually heard their repeated calls: "keee-keee-krrrt-krrt-krrt." (Footnote Five)

The birds, a national Bermudian symbol, are aptly named because their tails, over two feet long, stick out from their two and a half foot bodies. And, their pointed wings are even four or so inches longer than their bodies. Jet black strips of color show on their breasts and both their wing tips. The underside of their wings near their bodies has triangular black shapes like Bermuda Island.

"The birds come to shore between April and October for nesting. They nest in crevices and holes, and lay a single egg. When not breeding and during the winter they wander & fly far out into the ocean. The birds plunge and feed on fish and squids," says www.bermudaattractions.com.

Within two days, Christopher sailed into Bermuda harbor after 12 previous days in the ocean; only two days longer than he figured the trip would take. He first spotted Bermuda's famous North Rock at the edge of its reefs! It was mildly warm in the 80 degree range.

Sunny Bermuda from the air, even with swarming clouds, is a riveting three quarters of a circle-view. It is surrounded by green land dotted with mostly white roved residences and businesses. Its bright blue surface water is accentuated by a huge, light brown coral reef with white sands below. That's all surrounded by darker, deeper blue waters moving out into the ocean depths.

Christopher's sail boat was immersed in two tone blue wavy waters. From his perch, he could see light blue, green and red homes covered with super bright white roofs, and their special gutters, constructed to catch fresh drinking water. It was such a welcome site to Christopher, after surviving the dangerous storm, and after being so many years away from his childhood home.

"The North Rock is the largest coral reef in Bermuda" says Bermuda-Attractions.com. "This shallow coral reef covers an area with a 1000-meter radius from the North Rock Navigational Beacon. It was actually a land mass and could be visible above the surface even till early 1900's. But as the sea levels have risen with time, the reef has gone below the waters...The area around the North Block navigational beacon has been the graveyard for many ships. (Those) ships heading towards the navigational guiding light at North Rock, met their ill fate on the shallow blind Mills breaker reefs, which are to the south-east of North Block."

But, of course, Christopher, a veteran Bermudian sailor, most significantly was in familiar, calm and friendly waters now. From this point, he radioed Bermuda's Harbor Radio to give his location. At Christopher's request, a radio operator immediately called Christopher's brother, Peter.

In total surprise to Christopher, not long afterward, Peter motored in a power boat out from Bermuda's harbor to North Rock. Aboard with him were a reporter and photographer from The Royale Gazette newspaper. As Christopher continued to manage his sails and the tiller, and the motor boat cruised alongside, he excitedly greeted his brother. Soon afterward, as the two boats moved forward, the Gazette reporter interviewed him and the photographer snapped a bearded, long-haired Christopher, smiling and waving while standing inside "One Day."

Christopher Profit waves from his sail boat as he is photographed by Tony Cordairo, photographer for The Royal Gazette.

The first words out of Christopher's shouting mouth, says The Gazette report, were: "I made it!" Next, the Gazette quoted Brother Peter as reacting: "It's called the "One Day," because one day he was going to do it!" Peter then called his brother 'a life-long dreamer,' the newspaper story says.

Once they docked, got off the boat and moved inside customs, Christopher met up with those who had been inside a 100 foot boat in the same ocean. "They told him of the horrors of being thrown around during the storm. I had no idea how hard it was (for such a large boat) until I talked to them."

Earlier, the reporter quizzed Christopher only about the larger details of his storm experiences without getting the most fascinating gem, Christopher's hands on experiences with the friendly, companion swallow.

During the interview, the motor boat, making its buzzing noises, and the sail boat continued to move toward the harbor. "I was sailing, and still concentrating on sailing," he says. So only the basic storm crisis at sea, Christopher says, got the attention.

Later, he says, he did tell the bird in hand tale to his fellow Alcoholics Anonymous members at one of their meetings. And, the story did get out by word of mouth to others, including Stephen West, the Bermudian artist. He enjoys painting wild creatures and the interaction among those wild critters and humans. It was Stephen who first made this author aware of the story, seven years after that drama occurred.

But such wild bird landings on boats at sea do happen, according to an article by Dave Grant, entitled "Cetaceans, Sharks and Songbirds," discussing whale watches off Cape Cod. Here's part of his tale!

"Species that landed on the deck (and on the heads, shoulders, and cameras of fearless American Littoral Society whale-watchers), included: orioles, white-throated sparrows, and at least six species of warbler: redstart, magnolia, myrtle, black and white, yellow, and parula. They appeared quite tame, owing to their exhaustion; which is odd since we were never that far from land." (Footnote six)

Imagine that! These wild birds actually landed on the heads and shoulders of seafarers!

What's more birds have enlivened sailors at sea for hundreds of years. Here's an excerpt from Christopher Columbus' sailing log from the southern Spanish seaport Palos out toward the Canary Islands. It generates from the Franciscan Archives.

"Christopher was then in command of three ships: the Niña, the Pinta and the Santa Maria. It was Thursday 20 September 1492: "Two pelicans came on board, and afterward another, a sign of the neighborhood of land. Saw large quantities of weeds today, though none was observed yesterday. Caught a bird similar to a grajao; it was a river and not a marine bird, with feet like those of a gull. Towards night two or three land birds came to the ship, singing; they disappeared before sunrise." (Footnote seven)

But to Christopher, his swallow sailing companion seemed not so routine or startling or exotic as it did inspirational. "To this day," Christopher says, "I can still feel the tiny feet of the swallow on my left hand."

Christopher's new life in Bermuda, a land filled with singing, crying, flying and perching birds, was just beginning. He found the successive boat crafting jobs he had been looking for throughout his adventures. In fact, it would be 15 years before he would move away the island that welcomed him after the long-ago tropical storm. Today he lives in Ontario, Canada.

After that death defying experience, blessed by the extraordinary bird's landing on his hand, Christopher exclaims: "It changed my life in that I now live in the moment."

Footnote one: http://en.wikipedia.org/wiki/Marine_automobile_engine#cite_note-7

Footnote two: http://www.nauticalcharts.noaa.gov/nsd/distances-ports/distances.pdf

Footnote three: http://bermuda.omnimystery.com/

Footnote four: http://www.bermuda-triangle.org/html/the_disappearance_of_flight_19.html

Footnote five: http://en.wikipedia.org/wiki/White-tailed_Tropicbird

Footnote six: http://ux.brookdalecc.edu/staff/sandyhook/dgrant/field/CC-Whalewatch.htm

Footnote seven: http://www.franciscan-archive.org/columbus/opera/excerpts.html

A big, beautiful Monarch Butterfly became one of several wild creatures that inspired a young man, Peter Litwin, to believe there are spirits within all living beings connecting them in inspiring ways so long as they heed the signs.

A Farm Boy Becomes a Spiritual Man of Nature

Some noise, some movement or maybe even some instinct made the farm boy in his early teens look up in the clear blue sky on a beautiful sunny fall day with the leaves gleaming through the tree branches in full color.

"There hovering in the breeze was the albino red tailed hawk," says Peter with excitement. "The sunlight came through all of the feathers of the hawk. I remember being awestruck by the beauty of its feathering. The sunlight on the other side of the feathers of the hawk created almost like an X-ray vision of this bird...I could see it's wing bones, and I could see its sort of skeleton framework mostly on the wings through the sunlight which filtered through the feathers. I was awestruck by it, and somehow at that moment, there was a connection in a most profound and deep way between the bird, between me and the sun and the whole indescribable beauty of the experience."

Now in his 60s, Peter A. Litwin, that former teen, still lives on Arbutus Farm in Litchfield, Connecticut, near that very same spot where he describes catching sight of that albino hawk some five decades ago. He and his wife, Eileen, dwell on a hill in the midst cattle and hay fields, several small forests and several man made ponds.

From their historic, well-preserved New England red clapboard house, they can walk 75 yards higher up on a hilltop to a rock overlook. On top, the landscape seemingly travels to the infinity of long hay fields and woods upon woods. Peter and Eileen have partied up there with friends on beautiful days or evenings in all warm seasons. Other times they just amble up for a horizon-filling, southerly view of fields, ponds and trees. More recently and mostly yearly, if the weather holds, Eileen hosts a sunrise Easter service on that potentially windy, chilly high nature chapel. Lower down on property on the northwest side of Litwin Road, Peter has created a cosy little wild bird sanctuary with plenty of houses.

When Kate and Nate, two of their children were young, the Litwins temporarily adopted a crow, and then a summer or two later, a three-legged buck.

One day, Peter visited a livestock dealer in Morris and spotted two baby crows in a cage. The dealer told him he captured them because he thought of them more as pests than birds.

Peter immediately worried about the fates of those babies. He asked if he could purchase them. The dealer insisted that he could sell only one. Peter, wanting to free both, reluctantly agreed. The Litwins soon named the black-feathered fledgling Charlie. They fed him daily. Holding yellow scrambled egg batter in their fingers, they eased it down the little bird's throat. "He loved the eggs," says Peter. Charlie regularly perched and rode on everyone's shoulders. He flew around nearby when one or more of the Litwins explored the farm or the neighborhood.

"We had a wonderful experience with Charlie. (He) was smart and taught us a lot," says Peter. About six months after Peter obtained Charlie, he began hanging out with other crows. Eventually, Charlie flew off with a flock of crow buddies and never returned.

Peter holds his crow sculpture, inspired by his love of birds.(Photographer Unidentified)

A year or two later in the summer, the Litwins were upset when they heard a buck was hit by a neighboring farm hay cutter's blade and lost its back right leg. The incident happened in a hay field, not far from their own. Soon afterward, the Litwins, discovering the baby buck might be mercy-killed by a veterinarian, adopted him. They eventually revived the little one fully by feeding him goat's milk from a bottle. He became known as Hero.

"The most spiritual, loving animal you could imagine," says Peter. "Hero would come up and suck your ear lobe like he was nursing." He was everyone's playful pet for about six months before he gradually became more independent, slept in the garden and began hiding under a big squash leaf. "He'd pop out and run around like a puppy, and we'd chase him. Even with three legs, he didn't slow down. You would never catch him," Peter says.

Finally, the growing juvenile buck began disappearing into the woods to hang out and socialize with other deer. Eventually, like Charlie The Crow, Hero disappeared into the wild. Two years later, says Peter, friends in Litchfield showed them a videotape of an eight-point buck with its back right leg severed. "We were absolutely certain it was Hero," says Peter.

It was Peter's namesake grandfather, along with his grandmother, Tekla, who first bought and farmed the family property in the 1920s, utilizing a horse team and a hand held plough. Decades later, Peter's, the younger's father, Theodore, and his mother, Martha, took over.

The Litwin's Arbutus Farm began its history as the Catlin-Goslee Family Farm in the last quarter of the 1700s. Before then, it was, like all of its surroundings, American Indian country.

Once Peter's mother and father slowed their farming chores down, he continued work the land as a second job. Initially, an attorney-partner for a Litchfield firm, he eventually created his own small law partnership to help Eileen, a massage therapist, keep bread in the oven for Kate, Nate, and the youngest child, Josh.

Since his birth, Peter has never abandoned one form of working the farm or another. As a youth, and the only son with two sisters, he worked with his father on that dairy farm operation with Golden Guernsey cows.

"I was alone a lot in my life (while) growing up on this farm. Experiencing nature first hand became a platform for my life," says Peter. His father, he explains, is a close observer of nature and taught Peter about the wildlife scene. "We hunted and fished and always ate what we killed...We took only what we needed and never abused nature."

In one hunting adventure, Peter wounded a deer in the forest while hunting and it fled. It took him hours, while chasing through field and stream, before he finally caught up to the wounded one so he could now mercy kill it.

"As I grew older, says Peter, "I developed an intimate relationship with nature that changed my life. I learned and understood there was a connection between all living things. For me the birds and the animals are my brothers and my sisters. I feel I can communicate with them. I think they communicate with us. You just must have the patience and the wisdom to understand them and live in harmony with them."

Peter and Eileen are both focused on the spiritual in life, and took several introspective courses to deepen their faiths and souls. Eileen is devoutly religious, while Peter is not, but believes in the metaphysical or the spirits at the heart of nature. "I'm not a religious person. My spirituality evolved from these experiences I had on the farm. These experiences are the foundation of my belief system," he says.

Eventually, Peter says, his mind searching led him to believe his soul is appearing as a "gentile-faced, crinkly old (American) Indian called White Hawk." Peter's riveting episode with the albino hawk, a creature he had never seen before and has not seen since the two or three years it hung around the neighborhood, is still in his memory bank, almost as fresh as yesterday.

"It was unmistakable. It was pure white. It would show up against virtually any background except snow. I remember watching it almost every day. A lot of people (came) over to the farm to see it through binoculars. Initially, I don't remember it with a mate, but as it stayed a couple of years, it did have a mate. They would fly together and sit together. It was really quite a sight! I was entranced by this bird. I would look for it all the time, and constantly follow it with my eyes. I would try to get as close as I could. There was something about it that was just magnetic. I had incredibly close encounters."

Peter's most memorable experience came when he was hunting on a sunny, beautiful fall day inside the colorful leafy forest. He instinctively looked up to see it floating in the breezy blue sky. It mesmerized him. Peter felt he could see into the bird's soul, as the sun's ray's seemed to pierce its body.

"It was that type of experience and others that made me feel a direct union and a direct connection with the bird, particularly and perhaps more importantly, with all living things; because, we were farmers," Peter explains." We lived from the land, cared for all our own animals, our vegetables and our and fruits. We cut wood for heat. We really lived life on the land in a way that is almost hard for anyone who is not a farmer to understand. But, we have this very, very deep, daily life-sustaining connection and that wasn't an easy relationship all the time."

"There were storms. There was hardship. You had hay down and it got wet and caused a lot of extra work. (Storms) caused lots of crops to fail. So there was sort of an up and down equation between nature and us. But the long and the short of it was that we knew we were part of nature and nature was part of us. We lived a life where the seasons and the rotations of the sun had a direct and immediate impact on almost everything that we did."

There were many other experiences with animals and birds out in the wild near his farm that Peter cherished. "They made me become a little wild child in some way because I would sleep in the woods and I would (walk and explore) in the woods in the dark," he says. "I loved to go in the woods during a storm. There were lots of times we weren't working and I was free to roam. I saw a lot of the country. I knew other brooks and valleys. I knew a lot of the trees - just being with them so much," Peter explains.

When Peter reached his late teens, he began to assume a greater role on the farm. He started tractoring, cutting hay, gathering it up and stacking it in the barn. One summer's day, Peter had an experience which he explains "made all of my early learnings about nature and my feelings about it more intense and greatly magnified."

Here's the magic tale Peter tells:

"On a beautiful hay-day with a blue sky and fleecy white clouds, I was raking the south meadow. The hay was almost ready. I was just going to turn it over one last time with the rake, and then hurry quick to get the baler on the tractor and bail it. So it was just an intense and exhilarating afternoon."

"As you drive the tractor along (in the fields), you always see swallows in big flocks swirling around and around the tractor because the insects (were) stirred up by the tractor and the hay equipment. And you would often see hawks and mice and fox and woodchucks. There would be a fair number of butterflies. "

"On this particular day, at this one moment, (I spotted) a Monarch butterfly totally captivating my attention. The butterfly was probably flying 12 to 15 inches from my face on the right hand side as I drove the tractor down the row. I was going along pretty good because again this was the last time around just to tip the hay one last time. The butterfly was keeping pace with me - right there close by – when all of a sudden, it just landed on my upper right arm. I wasn't wearing a shirt. I just (wore) little cut off jeans."

"It's not often that you have a butterfly land on you. So this was very unusual...It stayed right there as I was driving along on the tractor...It became clear to me that this butterfly was my grandfather, Peter Litwin...come back to me to see me and to commune with me, to spend time with me. How this came into my mind, my consciousness I don't know. It doesn't really matter. It was unmistakable. It was unshakeable."

"The butterfly and my grandfather's spirit rode with me around the field for a long time. When I say a long time, I'm not talking hours...but minutes. It's never happened like that before or since. It was very clear to me that it was my grandfather, Peter."

"He was there with me, and even beyond that, it was a warm flow of feelings between him and me. He was thankful that I was on the farm taking care of the land; that I was raking the hay and cutting the fields, and basically taking care of things. It was most prideful for him and for me really because I felt acknowledged...in a very warm and embracing way, connecting with my grandfather who had been dead for some years."

"After a time, I don't remember exactly how long, the butterfly...went his way. It was exhilarating! It was a very complete experience. There was nothing that needed to happen to make it more than it was. It was unforgettable," Peter concludes.

From that experience, the way he lived previously and was brought up by his family, says Peter, "I formed a very concrete feeling that there was a spirit of all things beyond myself and all around me all the time, and that nature represented kinship, and kinship not only of all those we know, but all those who have gone before us, both human other creatures (in the wild)."

Peter came to believe that all living beings have a common heritage, a common path, a common energy in one universe and one earth together. "Other experiences I have had since just intensified that. Even now, wherever I go, I constantly watch for birds and animals, and for fish. It's kind of a joke with my family because I'm always saying: 'Look at the hawk! Look at the heron! Look at the bear!' Most people don't understand how I can see them (so easily)," he exclaims.

While Peter occasionally saved a deer or a crow from potential tragedy, Susan Dwyer made the dramatic rescue of baby animals into a loving career.

The Saviour of Baby Wild Animals of All Kinds

Susan Dwyer, has, perhaps, become a single-handed mother to as many injured or sick baby wild animals as any human being can possibly be. She rescues them from near death: at the paws and claws of dogs; perilous falls from trees and rocks; the loss of their own moms in the forest; and, from mysterious and untold brutal adventures in the wild.

In her eleven years of daily off and on 24 hours of nursing, the one-woman intensive care unit has gone from handling 100 baby animals annually to 445 in 2009 to over 600 a year later. These baby raccoons, possums, squirrels, foxes, skunks and other assorted new-borns require her to feed, nurse, caress and talk to her little furry patients hourly, a lot of the day and a lot of the night. She sets her alarm repeatedly at night to awake and continue animal care.

In the past, that meant that she transported all of her brood by car from her home in Granby to her regular job as a state computer systems administrator in Hartford. There she was able to fit in regular feeding and nursing visits to their nursery containers in the state's parking garage. "I must have had the best travelled babies around," Susan says.

More recently, she obtained volunteer help so the babies can stay at home.

"There is something addictive about rehabbing animals, especially the babies," says Susan. " Their lives literally depend upon you. With the help of a higher power we are able to save many of these little lives in our care. This year I have a real nursery and a couple of wonderful volunteers who feed the babies during the day so can I leave them home."

Baby nursing season normally starts mid-March to early April and ends the end of October. However, the weather plays a pivotal role in determining when wild moms have their babies.

When it is a mild winter followed by an early spring, babies can start arriving in Dwyer's nursing care as early as late January or early February. When there is a mild fall and a late winter, baby season can extend well into November and even to December.

"December is the month to get some sleep and catch up on everything I missed since the baby season began," Susan explains. "Soon it will be January, and time to prepare for another baby season."

Her general interest in wild critters started when she was five-years-old, but since then, she has spent hours on end helping out injured baby animals.

"I have always loved animals since I was a little girl," Susan says. "I lived in the country and there were animals all around me. My happiest times occurred walking through the woods and watching all the plants and animals around me. I would always go into the woods, find a brook, and look into the water to see the fish and the turtles. My brother would go with me. I took a lot of photos when I was 9 or 10 years old. I frequented the back yard and the pasture. We, my brother and I, always grew up this way. That was our entertainment."

"The animals are fascinating to watch as they busily go about their daily lives. It is wondrous how much knowledge Mother Nature has endowed them with so they can survive."

"By the time I was a teenager it was a routine for several raccoons came to the back door of our house. I got a bunch of cookies and fed them. One day, a little raccoon came back with his two front paws injured. His feet were bleeding with wounds down to the bone. I cleaned his paws and made a bed for him. I talked to him the whole time I was caring for him. He gazed into my eyes trustingly, and didn't object even when I had to put disinfectant and antibiotics on his wounds. He was unable to use his paws so I fed him. Then he curled up and went to sleep."

"He slept during the day and disappeared when it got dark. The next morning he would come back, and I would feed him, and he would go to bed. It took him a long time to heal. He was not able to defend himself, so he stayed away from the other raccoons, especially a mother with babies because they consider males a threat. "

"'Just give her a clear berth and stay away from her,' I told him. Later, when he was better, his routine would be to come to the back door and scratch it. I'd then give him a couple of cookies. He used to (stand up and) twiddle the buttons on my robe. It was good exercise for those little fingers that were still healing. His paws finally healed, but he always had scars so I knew which raccoon he was. He kept coming back for ten years. He got to be a ripe old age. I couldn't have been happier for those school years."

Susan's state computer systems job was becoming so intense, she says she needed another more enjoyable life to live. "I designed my computer systems seven days a week, 18 to 20 hours a day, for a year to finish the (new state) computer center. I was totally burned out and decided that life was too short to spend my life in a computer center. I decided it was time to do something for me," she says. "I always loved animals. I (obtained) my wildlife rehabilitator's permit so I could save orphaned wild babies."

"(Rehabilitating baby animals) is the most demanding, stressful and frustrating thing I have ever done, (but) it is also by far the most rewarding. There is nothing like watching them grow up into beautiful juveniles or adults. When they are ready to go back to the wild, I take them out to their release site. 'You go ahead and have a good life and be safe,' I tell them. Most rehab people don't spend the time I do with the babies because it is too intense for them," explains Susan.

"Many times they come in here in such terrible condition. The most I can do for some is to make them comfortable. They go to bed in a warm fleece blanket with a full tummy and something for discomfort or pain. Some go to sleep and don't ever wake up. Sometimes I will rock them for a while. That's the downside of rehabbing, losing them while they are in your care. You go and get a few minutes sleep and then wake up to check on them and they are gone."

"When a baby first (arrives), they are in an intensive care ward until they are stabilized. (That) can take up to 3 days or more. A rehab nursery is an intensive care unit, emergency room, isolation ward and a rehabilitation ward, all rolled into one. They have to be stabilized for 25 hours. It's normally 3 days in intensive care. Once they are stable, they go into the nursery. Families are kept together. We could get from two or three siblings up to a whole litter of 14 to 18 opossum babies."

"My first baby (assignment) arrived on Mother's Day," Susan says. "Someone called about a baby flying squirrel. She brought the baby over, and there was a baby about the size of the end of your finger. I remember holding him in my hand and saying to my self, 'Oh my God, how am I even going to feed this baby?' Then I remembered the cup of supplies that Chris (Christina Clark) at the Squirrels & More store prepared for me (earlier). I ran to get the cup, and dumped the contents on the table. There was one tiny pipette that looked like it might work. Nothing else even came close. I prepared his formula and tried feeding him with the pipette. It worked! It just fit in his tiny mouth."

"He was hungry and ate all the formula, which at that size was about six drops a feeding. At that size he needed to be fed about every half hour around the clock. New rehabbers tend to be scared to death of losing a baby. I was no exception. We had some tense moments, but he stabilized and Rocky grew up to be a handsome flying squirrel."

One of Susan's most emotional rescues started from a police complaint. This is what she wrote about it:

"In late June 2006, I received a phone call from the Hartford Police. A gentleman in the North End called to report that during his early morning walk he had found a baby raccoon stuck in a fence. The policeman drove to the man's house with me. The man had a nine-week-old baby raccoon in a box. The baby was just barely moving. As I picked her up and moved her to my transport carrier, the gentleman told me there was a family of raccoons that came around every night."

"The babies were just large enough to follow their mom. The neighbor had a large Rottweiler watchdog that had been trained to be mean. The babies must have wandered into the neighbor's yard and ran when the dog startled them."

"The baby, I named Angel, made the mistake of trying to get through the chain link fence and got stuck. Unable to free herself, she endured the rest of the night with the dog snarling and lunging to grab her. She was just inches out of his reach. While she didn't have any physical injuries other than some bruises from trying to force herself through the chain link fence, her mental condition was a different matter."

"Raccoons are extremely intelligent, and they suffer from some of the same mental conditions that we do. By the time I got her home, she had completely withdrawn and was unresponsive. I treated her for extreme fear, with limited success."

"Wild animals will go into a trance-like state when faced with extreme fear. Each species has its own limit as to how much fear they are able to tolerate before this happens. She began to acknowledge me and would hold my finger when I fed her with a glass liquid dropper, but no more than that."

"All animals handle stress differently. Bunnies with stress just drop dead on you. But a raccoon goes into trance. Her lack of response made me decide to treat her for PTSD. Post traumatic stress disorder is not limited to people. Imagine spending hours with a huge vicious animal a couple of inches away trying to rip you apart. "

"Angel began responding to hands on care within two weeks. I began talking to her. I saw her eyes moving. She would watch me feed her. The second week she would hold my finger with her paw. A week after that she began to sit up and eat on her own. Three months later, I said goodbye and wished Angel a happy life as I released her in a wooded park away from people and dogs. I put out food for her. She came back after a while."

"Then she went out for about a month and a half. When she reappeared, she had grown into a big, beautiful raccoon. After initially seeing me, she briefly went back into the woods, came back and brought five beautiful babies with her for Grandma to see. It was like she was thanking me"

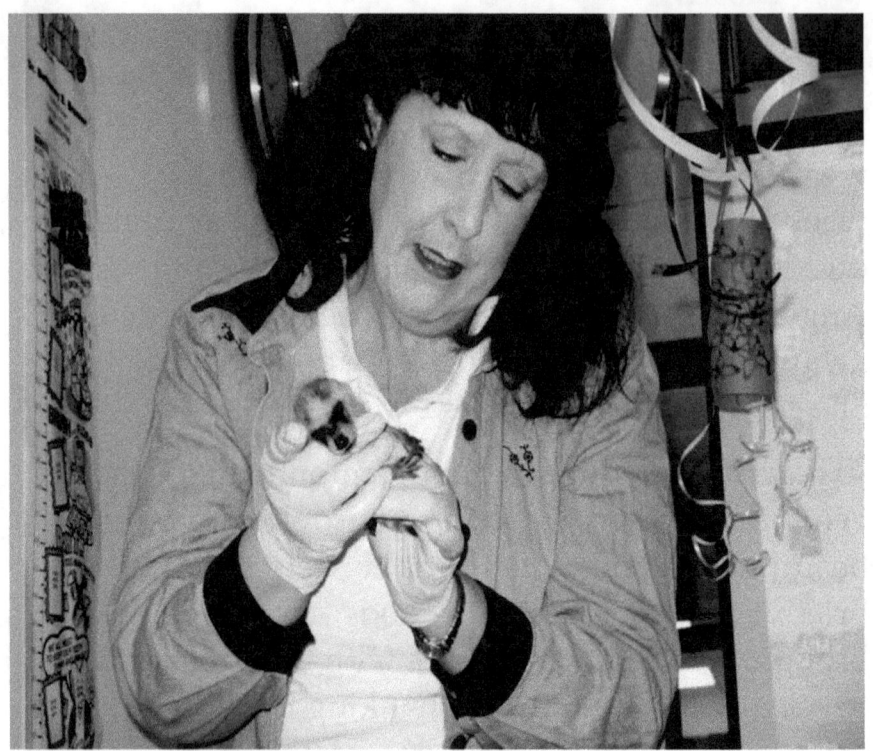

Susan saves and nurses a baby raccoon. (Photographer Unidentified)

Before Susan became an animal rehabilitator, several other inspiring experiences made her a believer in the extraordinary powers of all wild creatures to interact and communicate with humans who are sensitive to nature's spiritual dynamism.

About 17 years ago, says Susan, she went whale watching in a rubber Zodiac boat at the San Ignacio Lagoon, which is in the Baja Peninsula in Mexico. It is the grey whale nursery on the west coast.

"It was hit or miss to spot them," Susan explains. "It was bad timing. We had hardly seen any during the whole trip. The last morning, we took one last trip out in the Zodiac. It was a grey overcast morning and the sea was calm. There wasn't a sound."

"Then, out of nowhere, up (out of the sea) pops a baby grey whale. It leaned around and over the rounded and flexible boat side and put its chin on my lap and opened his mouth. It looked at me for a minute. There were four other people in the Zodiac with me, and we were all speechless. 'What do I do now?' I remember thinking. I could lose my arm, but I didn't think so. I leaned over and put my hand on the baby whale and petted it."

The baby retreated for a short stint under water, she explains, but then again popped up over boat side to put its chin into her lap. This time, she says, she decided to get even friendlier.

"I started rubbing his gums and he was shivering to my touch," she says. "I could feel the baleen plate starting to come up through the gums. The baby was teething. He stayed about five minutes in the ocean around us circling, and blowing bubbles, sounding like the boat motor. After a few minutes of rubbing, the baby whale went below and swam around the Zodiac making a sound that sounded exactly like our outboard motor. He did that a few times and then returned to my lap for more gum rubbing."

"All the time the mother whale was about 15 feet under our Zodiac motionless. It must have been about a half hour before mom surfaced next to us. Baby joined her, and a moment later, they were swimming away. It was just as though mom took baby out to play and playtime was over. Now they had to be on their way."

"My husband managed to lean over me to get one photo of me petting the baby, but everyone was too captivated by the baby to remember to take pictures the rest of the time. "

If you do not believe this can happen, here is a direct quote from an Internet posting with photos from "Lynn, Laura, Eloise and me" writing on "Baja Dreaming":

"It's an experience that entered my psyche, bounced around my emotional pool and exited through my intellect. Soft whale skin pressed against my cheek. A throat lifted toward me – 'please scratch me.'"

"Mother whales lifted babies toward the boat. This gift, this play, this sharing: Can it not be considered an act of love? How is it possible that these extraordinary leviathans trust us at all? Hunted to near extinction – not once, but twice – their numbers had been reduced to fewer than 100 by human hands hungry for lamp oil. That they continue to reach out to us, present their young for petting, acknowledge and seek out our presence is a mystery – and some would call, a miracle." (Footnote one)

Susan Dwyer's experience was not enough for her. "Four years after that first trip," she says, "we took another whale trip to the Sea of Cortez in Mexico. We had not seen much the whole trip in a cabin cruiser. There were fifteen other people in the boat with us."

"One nice afternoon, we were heading to shore when someone hollered: 'Hey look over in front of us! What kind of a whale is that?' Then a crew member said, 'I don't believe it! That's a Blue Whale!' We watched it feeding. It dove in the fairly shallow water, came up on its back and breached, landing back in the water on its back. As it breached (the ocean) and fell backward, we could see the water rushing through the baleen pates like a waterfall before it crashed back into the water and righted itself to prepare for the next dive. As it righted itself, it spotted us."

"Curiosity took over. It watched us for a short while. Then it headed toward us. There was a moment of concern when we saw how much larger it was than our boat. It gracefully slipped past the bow and swam alongside; then turned around and swam alongside back toward the bow. As it came alongside, it leaned slightly over on its side and looked up at us. It was curious and decided to check us out. It is an indescribable feeling when you look in the eye of a Blue Whale. He hung around a bit and then went on his way. I took pictures of him with an 8 millimetre camera," Susan says with excitement of her photographic proof.

As exciting as her rare socialization with these whales was for Susan, it could not match the more intimate and loving experiences she had with the horse of her dreams, Spotter, a leopard-spotted mare.

Here is Spotter's tale first hand from Susan:

"It was an Indian-style Appaloosa I rescued from a riding school at a nearby farm when he was sixteen. I boarded him at the farm for a few years until I had a barn built at home. Horses need exercise, even in the winter, so in bad weather, I took him in the large riding arena and exercised with a lunge line. It is a very long rope or canvas reinforced lead line hooking onto hooks the horse's halter. The horse then moves in a circle around the person at various gaits. We were exercising like this when some snow suddenly slid off the metal roof, making an awful noise. Spotter was startled and jumped sideways. It was just a small jump, but it was enough to yank me off my feet."

"Spotter was satisfied there was no danger, and was ready to resume. He looked over at me as I lay on the ground with the lunge line wrapped around both hands. He stood there for a minute, waiting for me to get up. When I didn't, he walked over to me and put his head down near my face. He then walked around beside me, and put his head under my elbow (and arm) and (gradually) lifted me up until I could get my feet under me. I had no way to undo the clasp on the lunge line with broken fingers on both hands. So he put his head over my shoulder and walked back to the nearby barn with me."

"Someone was in the barn, took Spotter's lunge line off and put him back in the stall. Every day, after that, I went to visit him. He (insisted upon staring at) my fingers and smelling them. The day I went to see him after I got my splints off, he looked at my fingers and smelled them again. His eyes got bright and he pranced around his stall. He knew I was OK again, and we were going riding. I put him in the cross-ties to saddle him. He was dancing around so much I didn't know if I could get the saddle on. I finally prevailed. Off we went with his head held high and mane and tail flying in the breeze. He was so happy."

"The next spring we went to a horse show. Spotter had ribbons for just about everything, (even though) I had never competed with him before. When it was our turn, he knew just what to do, but I didn't handle the jump correctly. I fell off. The emergency (medical) crew ran over to keep me still until they could get me on a board in case I hurt my back or neck."

"Meanwhile, a crew of people ran to catch Spotter before he ran off and hurt himself. As I was put in the ambulance, I looked out to see Spotter standing at the ambulance door. He didn't take off; he was trying to get into the ambulance with me. It took several people to hold him back."

"Fortunately I only sustained some bad bruises and went to see Spotter the next day. I walked into the barn to see him with his head down, looking very depressed. He looked up as I opened the stall door and his eyes brightened up. He came over and gave me a (tongue) kiss on the cheek and nuzzled my neck. He was a very special horse."

"Shortly after that (episode), the barn was finished and Spotter came home for good. As he aged, he became almost blind, as many Appaloosas do. One day, I got a call at work. Spotter had gotten loose somehow and was no where to be seen. I hurried home fearing the worst. He couldn't see cars and if he was near a road he could be hit."

"As soon as I got home, I started walking up the street calling him. I was about one forth mile up the street when I heard something behind me. I looked around and here was Spotter coming toward me at a full gallop. He didn't see me and passed me. I called out to him and he stopped on a dime, turned around and walked up to me. He nuzzled me, and put his head over my shoulder, and we walked back down the street to the driveway and back up to the barn."

"I found out later that he had galloped all the way to the post office and back to my street without getting hit by a car. How he found his way back from the post office I will never know. He couldn't have heard me calling him from that distance."

"I had him for 29 of his 45 years. He passed away last summer in his sleep at that ripe old age of 45. Rest in peace my dear old friend."

Footnote one:
http://bajadreaming.wordpress.com/2008/02/21/whale-kissing-spy-hopping-in-baja/

While Susan Dwyer spends countless hours seven days a week saving animals, two other rescuers were called temporarily into one of the biggest environmental disasters in history to rescue all the wild creatures whose lives were threatened by the scary rush of oil below and above the surface of the Gulf of Mexico.

Saving Birds and Other Wildlife, A Spiritual Transformation

Just the sight of a Pelican waddling helplessly on the beach and dripping head to toe in black or orange brown crude oil is so horrifying it compels a nature lover to look away in hopes the images were simply a bad dream. Unfortunately, they were not!

"Those images, the news feeds, never left me. Sometimes I worked 20-hour days. Just seeing the pelicans covered in oil (on television and in person) made me feel I could go for another 21 hours," says Carissa Kent.

She was a bird and wildlife rescuer during the record, mammoth oil gush into the Gulf of Mexico. Kent, who lives in Oviedo, Florida, with David, her equally environmentally friendly husband, has had years of experience in voluntarily caring for both threatened wildlife and abused children.

She volunteered five years earlier to help the National Guard get flooded victims' pets out of their homes after the victims had been ordered to flee for their safety.

When she was a child, says Carissa, her grandfather inspired her readings of a variety of nature books. "You need to have that connection with nature," she says.

"There is a need for conservation education in schools: Just what you are doing with this book. There are not enough books out there that are main stream, and or accessible to public schools to teach this kind of conservation," Carissa explains.

So by the time Carissa grew into adulthood, she says, she became so acclimated to the wild, she found such predators as sharks and snakes to be much more fascinating than threatening.

"I always loved to play in the mud with earth worms and spiders and snakes, so I never had a fear of wildlife like some people do!" Carissa enthusiastically exclaims. Snakes took such a liking to her, she says, that she could intervene in dangerous situations and pick up and hold even poisonous snakes, threatening others. Sometimes she picked them up after they had just tried to strike at others.

"There are moments in your life when you can connect and tacitly communicate with wild creatures in nature, Carissa explains. "Then, you clearly see their purpose, and with any luck you may see your own." And, without predators, she says, their victims become overpopulated, leading to imbalance in forage, species and disease.

On April 20, 2010, Deepwater Horizon oil rig in the Gulf of Mexico, 52 miles southeast of the Louisiana port of Venice near the Mississippi River Delta, caught on fire and blew up. It killed eleven workers and injured 17 others on the rig. It created a 30-mile long black oil plume in the sky. The ugly, penetrating smell of burning petroleum soon penetrated environs all along the Louisiana coast.

About a week later, thousands of gallons continued to gush daily from British Petroleum's drill pipe below. Hundreds of workers tried futilely to control just the oil gush's thin slick tide and wave rush to shore with lengthy, but inadequate boom blockage.

Supervisors, seeing oil movement was impossible to control, set the slick on fire, creating more endless waterline smoke. Before the busted pipe source of one of the largest oil spills in the earth's history was contained, five months after it started, 205.8 million gallons had gushed into the ocean. The thick fluid blackened and destroyed shorelines, wetlands and overall environments of five states.

Recovery, if ever, will take decades. Generations of wild creatures can never develop as they had before the oil domination of their water and shoreline habitats.

Most of the news reports stressed the tens of billions in dollars of damage to coastal people-populated environments, and especially, fisherman's livelihoods as well as those of businesses in resort beach areas. However, relatively few stories focused upon the destruction of beautiful wild creature habitats, the fearful injuries and deaths of untold thousands of turtles, sea birds, fish and other wildlife.

Meanwhile, a large number of environmentalists and organizations including the Nature Conservancy, Conservation International, Environmental Defense Fund, Sierra Club and Audubon, worked on the spill's impacts on nature constantly for months. They became saviours of generations of wildlife, even as other birds, fish and animals were, perhaps, lost forever.

"I did not see the horror that was shown (close up) on TV. Rather, I saw the beaches and oil from a distance (in person). But, over all, the horror of it never left me," exclaims Carissa Kent, who worked six weeks on the crisis for Florida's Sumter Disaster Animal Response Team Inc. "We were involved in the oil bird rescue from Florida to Mississippi."

Although the horrifying wide angle or aerial scenes shown on television were not part of her team's observations, in person, she says: "I saw the birds and turtles soaked with oil and dying."

Carissa holding a saved turtle, one of her favorite sea critters. (Photographer Unidentified)

"When we were out of the boats, we could see birds that were clearly oiled; that were clearly ill. There are not a lot of (panoramas) around. We were then in Mississippi in the barrier islands out in the Gulf. There were actual pockets of oil around," Carissa explains with obvious pain.

Her glances from the boat, Carissa explains further, revealed mostly barren ocean with little vegetation growing on the islands.

"I was sitting there in the boat thinking this is so awful. We will never know the extent of this damage. I'm looking at one bird whose sick that we are trying to rescue...I was horrified. We were able to capture him. It was a Northern Gannet, a big white bird (covered in black oil slick) that spends most of its life at sea."

"All About Birds" describes the Gannets' normal activities and their beauty: "Flocks engage in spectacular bouts of plunge-diving for fish, with hundreds of birds diving into the ocean from heights of up to 40 meters (130 feet). It's a large water bird, white with black wingtips, a long pointed bill, and a long pointed tail and long pointed wings. Immatures range from all dark to mostly white." (Footnote one)

"This one was a juvenile," says Carissa. "He was just sitting on the beach. We were in the midst of doing actual recon. It was a call from the hot line (that alerted them to the bird). These are much protected islands that no one gets to walk on. They are endangered nesting sites protected by U.S. Fish and Wildlife, strictly inhabited by these species of birds. The Gannet was so obvious that we all saw it from quite a distance away. They are very large birds, quite beautiful and striking, very aggressive. He was just sitting there, kind of tilting back and forth on the shore."

"We beached the boat to get up and try to capture him while he was still on land. He let us walk up to him, which is very, very, very unusual. He kept bobbing, bobbing back and forth. You could see there was something wrong with him. He was oiled. He was sitting there. We got within a few feet of him. We had our nets out and attempted to capture him. He flew away, but poorly. He just fell into the water as he was flying. He couldn't fly more than 20 yards. He just crashed back in the water."

"We got into the boat, and within three minutes, maybe five minutes, we were able to manoeuvre (close to him). He was swimming. He tried to get up and fly, and he couldn't even fly. So obviously (the oil) had impacted his feathers. We were able to capture him. He was still trying to swim."

"The captain," she says, "pulled up close to him and cut the engine. We coasted right up beside him. My partner, a U.S. Food & Wildlife biologist and I carefully used our net to capture him and hoist him out of the water. We quickly placed him on the deck. I held the bird with think-gloved hands as the net was taken off of him. We placed an oil cloth inside a large dog crate, along with towels to support his breast bone and took him immediately back to shore and the rehabilitation center."

"There he was cleaned by rehabilitators from Tristate Bird Rescue & Research. That is a 34-year-old Newark Delaware based multidisciplinary team of wildlife biologists, veterinarians, pathologists, chemists and concerned citizens."

"The Gannet was stabilized on a soft oil cloth," Carissa explains. "Their breast bone is very, very delicate. You need to put enough towels and other protection on them to protect the bird's breast bone."

The big birds were fit into dog kennels to protect them from jostling up and down in the vehicles carrying them, and to protect those handling them from their aggressive nature, she says. "The Gannets could poke your eyes out. It is a very dangerous bird, but there was no such aggression toward us," Carissa explains.

Later, during a final transportation mission, Carissa continues, it happened by chance that she picked the cage of this very same juvenile Gannet in a Mississippi facility. "When I first saw him, I went: 'Ahhhhhh!' He was all healthy and happy. In all of the middle of this vast ocean, we found this one bird, and he made it!"

The bird was finally released into the Sun Coast Seabird Sanctuary, far enough from the spill so he could not return to his dangerous origins. Carissa and another woman picked up the heavy crate holding the bird. "We lifted up the sheet, and he kind of pecked at me," Carissa exclaims. "I think on my thigh, but not aggressively. And I went, 'Ohhh, I think I love you!' It was just like a little peck, because, if he wanted to hurt me (with a harder one), he could have."

"I felt a real connection being a part of that rescue, and I was almost in tears when we got him because it was spiritual, really. We were out in the middle of water with nothing else around there. The whole island and this bird and everything fit together so perfectly."

Carissa's second most memorable experience occurred as she and others were rescuing and releasing of two laughing gulls in the panhandle in Navarre, Florida.

"It has all kinds, tons of endangered species and nesting areas," she says. "It is the golden national seashore. It is gorgeous, absolutely gorgeous, very protected. There was a laughing gull just oiled and just wobbling again, basically falling over (on shore). It could barely fly. The team was there. I was there, as well, by the marina area where the boats come out. They took him and got to the rehab area."

"It was four or five days later," says Carissa, "when I got to release him. Before we started the release, we arrived at the beach, and set the crates down. We wanted it private and secluded."

"Once we took the crates out of the van, and walked them down to the beach, the gulls were not making any noise. Other laughing gulls flew in from the ocean, as we were walking down the beach itself to the point of the release, which was about 10 yards from the water."

"The gulls literally flew right by us and landed just a few yards off to our left. They waited there watching while we released the four gulls, two at a time."

"Then, those six or eight (observing) gulls flew around our heads and landed maybe ten feet away from us. They just sat there, and stared at us. They should never have been that close to us. They were just looking at the crate. You cannot see inside that dog crate. But, they could sense that rehabilitated gulls were being released. And yet, the gulls in the crates were not making any noise."

"When we took the top of the crate off," Carissa explains, "one just hopped out. It was amazing, and it was so funny, because when he got out, he kind of hobbled out. Normally, they just out hop out and just fly away. He turned around and he looked at me. He kind of had this funny expression on his face. He hopped around the crate, probably within a foot of me. He looked up at me."

"Then, his little buddy came around the crate to be with him. There were two in each of two crates. The four of them then walked over to the six others (waiting there for them), and they all flew off together into the sky. They circled around us for maybe a minute or two and flew out over the water. It was an amazing sight."

She had been extremely depressed at the very beginning of her six and a half weeks working in wildlife recovery in three Gulf States, says Carissa, because she had recently lost a solid full time job. Fortunately, she says, she was being paid by DART, as she did not have the financial resources to work as a volunteer. But her work around the Gulf reawakened her positive sensibilities.

"The depth of this experience was like nothing I had ever been through because of what it meant, not to me, but to the Gulf," Carissa explains. "It was part of a release effort and a response effort to one of our nation's most tragic moments, environmentally speaking. I remember before I left for the rescue, I felt so helpless. I have had many sleepless nights, as I am sure many people have, over the tragedy of it all."

"But to able to be a part of the effort that was making the situation better - for me that was the most fulfilling thing I have ever been a part of, because it worked."

"There were so many birds saved and so many turtles saved in this effort. If these people had come together, and it wasn't done so well; and everyone did not work together; and everyone did not have that passion and determination to save these animals (and birds), then they would not have had a chance. There are generations of birds and animals that were saved from this. But, obviously that is in addition to the tragic part that there have been generations that have been lost."

"I am proud to have been a part of an effort that helped save wildlife that was impacted by this," Carissa explains with obvious emotional tone in her voice. "It has forever changed me absolutely. It's something that has given me an even deeper appreciation for nature's Eco systems, because normally you don't think about the Eco systems in the Gulf that much. I think about everything that (lives) around here locally, the tortoises and this and that (creature) which I am involved with. But, we all forget there is a bigger world out there that we are connected to (and nature is connected to)."

Another of the Gulf of Mexico wildlife rescuers, Michael Pixley, became connected to nature for a lifetime at an early age. As a boy, he experienced constant and serious family problems that regularly drove him away from his rented farm home into the thick woods, dense swampland and beautiful countryside around Goshen, Connecticut. The modest wilderness became his refuge, a temporary escape from intensive conflicts at home.

"By the age of nine, my half brother Jon, six years older than me, had become the only positive male figure in my life, says Michael. "He often took me on hikes in the woods, and on fishing trips to places I was too young to go to on my own. Jon became, and still is, the most influential figure in my life. The outdoors became my safe place. It was the place I could be at peace with myself, and it was the place where I forged a bond with the only male influence every young man needs - desires. It was then and there that my lifelong relationship with nature began."

Jon and Michael liked exploring to find and play with salamanders, frogs and reptiles. Michael's first rescue in memory came when he was six. It was on one of those muddy, swampy trips that Jon and he discovered a large mouth Bass, floundering in shallow waters of a pond. They were able to catch it and move it to deeper waters nearby. But Jon, says Michael, saw the bass was still weak when he initially dropped it into the safer spot. So immediately, Jon picked it back up and found a nearby water current to hold the bass in, and give it oxygen. By hand, he moved it around in the water to revive it for a few seconds, before it swam off, explains Michael.

A year or so later during another wildlife excursion, says Michael, they discovered a wounded baby grey squirrel on the ground. It was laying on the edge of a cornfield next to a pasture adjacent to a wooded area. The corn had been cut and reduced to stalks six inches high. The baby, who couldn't seem to move at all, was about the size of the top of a metal soda can, says Michael.

They poked a stick at it. It moved, but appeared helpless so they took it home.

"We put it on the front porch and showed it to mother, explains Michael. Later, Jon and Michael moved the little fellow into the garage for safekeeping. Their mother got some goat's milk, and regularly fed it. The three cared for the squirrel for two weeks before freeing it into the woods.

Michael, now 30 years old, says he can never forget these two wonderful lifesaving experiences for those wild creatures. In fact, says he, they helped inspire him to become a professional saviour for animals, birds and water living creatures, like turtles and fish.

"I have always had issues in school with paying attention," says Michael, "or being able to study, or understanding classroom material. However, while outdoors, I never experienced a greater focus, being clear minded or, at peace. I wanted to know about everything in the woods. I wanted to know what everything (in the wildlife world) was about, how they worked together, and why!"

Michael, after graduating from high school, became an Athens, Georgia, resident, He was still finishing up a science and forest resources degree at the University of Georgia, when he got hooked. Simultaneously, he became a four-year veteran worker for the U.S. Fish and Wildlife Department. He was still finalizing his degree, when he was sent on the mission of his life.

Within a day or two of his own volunteer, but paid, federal assignment to BP's gigantic oil spill in the Gulf of Mexico, Michael Pixley, wearing personal protective equipment and rubber gloves, spotted his favorite species of turtle in distress on a freshly oil soaked cove in Barataria Bay, Louisiana.

"I looked (out from the boat) and I saw a Diamondback Terrapin. It just happened to be my favorite turtle. What is unique about these (tortoises) is that they are the only turtle that lives in brackish water. (This one) was about the size of a football and weighed two or three pounds," says Michael. The rescue was unforgettable, he insists, because it was his first wild creature rescue ever of the species of turtle he most enjoys.

"It wouldn't go in the water, obviously, because the whole shore was covered with oil. When we got to shore, I had hip waiters on. We beached (the small white motor boat). I jumped in (the water) and immediately sunk in to my waist. I am a big guy, about six foot five. That was three and a half foot of mud (I was wading in). I made my way toward it, but it didn't even try to run from me. I was able to grab it and pick it up. It was a rather large Diamondback female terrapin." The females are larger than their male counterparts.

"Diamondback turtles have concentric, somewhat diamond-shaped markings and grooves on the plates of their top shell, which ranges from medium grey or brown to nearly black. The feet are strongly webbed; the hind feet are especially large and flat," says Baltimore, Maryland's National Aquarium. (Footnote two) "Diamondbacks are well adapted for eating hard-shelled prey, including aquatic snails, crabs, and blue mussels. They also eat carrion, fish, marine worms, and plant material."

"It was probably about 10 feet from the water line," Michael explains. "The tide hadn't started to go out, but it was still relatively far away from the water line. Just knowing (the turtle) was outside of the water on land trying to hide, but not doing a very good job, (was a sign it was sick). These turtles are very secretive...and are actually pretty cool."

"Females require more calcium than males do," says Michael, "amounting to large amounts of calcium for egg production. They develop these large jaws for tearing at and eating oysters. They could very easily take my finger off. They are very beautiful turtles. There are ways you can grab them. Their nails will scratch you a little bit. I had gloves on, but she wasn't resisting very much. She was sick, definitely."

"Most turtles you pick up are going to resist. They are going to claw their way and hit back at you. She had her mouth open and she wasn't doing any of those things. She was lethargic. First thing we had to do was document where we found her," he explains.

Michael and others in the four-man boat took photos and made a written record of the rescue, including its coordinates and time, as they did with each of their captured wild creatures.

"We were making sure everything was safe for her, and then we transferred her to a cage, like a cat or dog crate. We taped around her (with cloth) so it was less stressful. It was very hot this day too, well over 100 degrees. We placed the crate in the boat in the back, securely, so it would not bounce around."

They radioed the rescue and its coordinates in to dispatch. Then, the boat motored off to veterinary mobile triage center, 45 minutes to an hour south. Usually, as in this case, Michael says, they took creatures individually straight there. If there were multiple birds to rescue, they might do so at the same time, if it was possible. Other times they called for an always readily available chase boat to take all the creatures they could not handle within their own craft.

Michael personally delivered this terrapin to the triage center for close emergency medical care. "I just remember they told me she had a little bit of oil on her," he explains, "but she was extremely dehydrated. That was an indicator that she was out of the water for a long period of time...sitting on land and baking herself because she did not swim into the oil slick. She was basically sitting in the hot zone getting cooked."

Michael got too busy to check on his favorite turtle, but he says someone at the triage center assured him 'she was going to make it.' He adds: "Getting confirmation she was OK from a professional, it was good...It is always a large sense of personal satisfaction, just knowing that you are helping."

The other startling rescue occurred when Michael's boat was carrying some interested representatives of the nature magazine, National Geographic. "I'd caught many birds at this point, I was considered a veteran. I was probably on week number six. We were looking at one of these small islands, probably an acre or two in size. It had multiple Brown Pelicans, Green Herons, and Terns that were covered in oil. We weren't going onto these islands because there was nesting there, and we didn't want to disturb those (scores of) birds (not endangered)."

Michael nets a sea bird, as his team readies to safely contain it, so the unidentified feathered one can be transported to a special medical care facility where it will be cleaned of oil and treated. (Photographer Unidentified)

"We were pointing out birds that were oiled. We had a communications line to report them in distress," he says. "Someone was calling in pretty close to us about an oiled Great Egret. The bird was probably a mile or two from us. It was floating out in the middle of the open water. So there's first the sign something was wrong."

"Great Egrets are wading birds. You don't find them floating out in the water like Terns and Pelicans. It was having trouble staying up and floating. Mostly what you saw was its head above water, held up with a big, long white neck. As I suited up in my white-back suit and got my gloves and boots on, we moved toward it with the boat."

"The Great Egret is a tall, large white egret," explains the Sungei Buloh Wetlands Reserve. "It is the largest that can be seen in (some nature reserves). It has extremely long legs and neck. Its neck is longer than its body, and is held in a distinctive kink."

"Great Egrets feed on mostly fish, but will also take amphibians (frogs), aquatic invertebrates (insects, crayfish), and reptiles (snakes). During the drier months, the bird will stalk small mammals, snails and nesting birds. But they prefer to steal food where possible. Great Egrets are skilled hunters. They stalk the shallow waters or mud flats, walking slowly or quickly with their strong neck coiled at ready."

"When suitable prey is spotted, they straighten out the neck to instantly snatch the prey. When fishing, they may tilt their heads to one side, possibly to avoid the glare of the sun's reflection on the water."

"Great Egrets may also use their feet to stir up the water and scare up a victim. When feeding in a flock, they may hop and leap frog to cut queue, when prey is spotted. They may even hover over, dip or plunge into the water while flying. Their feet are not webbed, but their weight is distributed over large feet so they don't sink in the mud. Although they happily roost with herons and egrets, Great Egrets hunt alone or in small, loose groups. Nevertheless, they usually vigorously defend a small feeding territory from other egrets," says Sungei Buloh Wetlands Reserve. (Footnote three)

As the boat captain accompanied by a biologist from the Louisiana Department of Wildlife and Fisheries steered toward the Great Egret, says Michael, "the bird actually turned and started swimming towards us. I was shocked because I knew something had to be wrong. It obviously wanted to be rescued for relief."

"There were points throughout the rescue where it could have been hostile, but again like the turtle," Michael explains, "it was lethargic, had extreme lack of energy and was exhausted. It tried to flap its wings a little bit, but in comparison to the some of the other birds that had oil on them, this one was very timid and drained of energy. At no point in time did the bird try to resist. If they, Egrets, weren't sick we could not have caught them. They are too energetic and quick."

"First thing when we brought her aboard, I grabbed her bill and head so she couldn't strike us in our eyes. He (the biologist) grabbed her other wing and untangled her feet from the net. I think it actually turned towards me (helplessly). It was in such despair. We opened the crate and then we both put her in," Michael explains.

He never found out whether the bird was male or female, says Michael. They filled out the necessary paperwork at the bird care center before leaving the scene. It included a description of the bird, the ocean conditions and the GPS coordinates. Radio dispatch had been alerted in advance to let triage personnel know the injured bird was inside the boat ambulance. The triage was the exactly same medical facility that had cared for the terrapin Michael rescued weeks earlier.

Michael says he carried the Egret's crate immediately to the veterinarians. Unfortunately, he explains, the doctors were completely overwhelmed and tired. So the doctors couldn't tell him what the egret's prognosis was. Numerous birds needing their attention were being delivered regularly every three or four hours.

"The Great Egret is one of 16 bird species threatened by the oil spill" according to thedailygreen, an Internet site. "Birds drenched in oil are one of the most moving and iconic images that result from oil spills. Looks can be deceiving, both because as few as one tenth of the birds affected by oil will ever wash up on shore, and because underwater plumes of oil could decimate marine ecosystems invisible to the human eye. That said: birds are among the most vulnerable creatures as the BP oil spill continues to spread in the Gulf of Mexico. In addition to oiled feathers, which destroys the birds' natural waterproofing; birds ingest oil directly or as part of a contaminated diet; or may experience oiled nesting, wintering or migratory habitat." (Footnote four)

Working seven days a week from 12 to 14 hours a day, starting at 6 a.m., Michael says he can never forget his two months of wildlife experiences in the Gulf. His area of assignment was the most attractive and populated for many bird species, because there are so many small protected nature islands for their nests. Just on Queen Bess Island alone, he explains, four and a half thousand to seven thousand nesting pairs of a variety of birds make their home.

For an hour and a half to two hours on all days, Michael says, he sat out on island perimeters just taking inventories of the juvenile birds nearby to discover that despite some of them being oiled, they were still being fed by their parents.

Michael's survival observances allowed delays in those particular bird rescues because Fish & Wildlife authorities understood they could wait for a significant period before capturing sick birds. The rescue delay allowed the nests of others, who were healthy, to be emptied, as the oil- free birds, sensing rescue efforts were ongoing, flew out to explore other areas.

In one instance, the calculated delay permitted Fish & Wildlife to save 28 oiled juvenile Pelicans, first inventoried by Michael, three weeks to a month earlier. Rescuers needed to allow oil to degrade and healthy juveniles the chance to fly elsewhere. By the time those 28 juvenile Pelicans were rescued, Michael had ended his Gulf of Mexico bird scouting assignments.

Fortunately, since rescuers were working in a warm water climate, birds, not severely oiled, could survive for days, says Michael. On the other hand, during the Exxon Valdez oil spill in Alaska in March 1989, the cold weather fatally froze oiled birds overnight.

Asked about his reaction to constantly saving oiled and damaged wildlife and observing despoiled plant life, ocean and beaches, Michael says: "I had good feelings. I had bad feelings. Obviously, I was devastated by the amount of wildlife I witnessed affected and habitat totally destroyed."

Already, he adds, the island habitats for bird nesting were being naturally eliminated by tidal erosion. They are in a vulnerable location near the Mississippi Delta where constant human dredging of ocean mud occurs. "These islands were naturally disappearing at an extremely rapid rate," he explains. When tides moved drifting oil onto island shores, it ultimately killed off natural wetlands' plant growth, including color-varying mangroves, allowing massive erosion to eliminate or diminish the islands.

But, on the other hand, he says: "The media spotlight is being shined on the disaster happening within the islands because of the oil spill. So that, in a sense, is a good thing." The public pressure may encourage BP and government funding in an attempt to save and restore many of the islands, he speculates. Decades earlier, there were some successful human efforts to bring in fill and plants to restore some eroded islands, he explains.

Actually, says Michael, he had worse reactions to BP and its oil explosion impacts when he arrived on the coast, then when he left. Once he observed developments, says Michael, he realized that BP workers, many of whom lived in the Louisiana area, were doing an amazing job helping people and the environment recover from the crisis. "Unlike their top BP bosses," he says, "they created hands on care, proving that despite their employer's negligence in causing the catastrophe; they worked long and hard to repair as much damage as possible. "

"BP corporate, the big wigs, the CEOs, those were the guys screwing up, but the people (BP workers) on the ground were trying their (butts) off to clean this, to fix this, to stop this. They were the ones that lived there," Michael explains.

On the way home, Michael had a mixed personal mindset, he says. "I felt like our efforts there, biologically speaking, when it came to saving these individual birds, weren't going to have much of an impact on the overall well being of the population, or the survivability of the population, I should say." However, he adds, there were countless severe impacts on the environment, habitats and other creatures, like fish, that could not be as easily observed as the birds were. So the deadly permanent damage is hard to measure, he says.

Indeed, Regis Trembley, director of Maine's Department of Inland Fisheries and Wildlife, says:

"Many birds that come here to winter or breed are 'in trouble' because of the human impact on their home ranges or their stop-over places as they migrate. For example, millions and millions of migrating birds use the Gulf of Mexico to refuel as they travel back and forth between Antarctica, South America, North America, and Canada. The oil spill in the Gulf of Mexico could deprive these migrating birds of the food they require to refuel as they continue their journeys. What effect this catastrophic disaster will have on the many ecosystems of North and South America, and on birds, fish, sea mammals, and plant life will not become obvious for years to come." (Footnote five)

But, if the impact of this spill is compared to that of the Exxon Valdez in Alaska, Michael explains, the latter was far more deadly to birds overall. Cold water and freezing air killed the feathered oiled ones quickly, while warm water in Gulf spared many oiled, sick birds, because the slick dried on their feathers, allowing some of them to move around and even fly.

Melonie Driscoll, writing in Audubonmagazine.com, in October 2010, says: "…it is too early to know what the impact of the Deepwater Horizon spill has been or will be on bird populations. We do know that the count of carcasses, and the number of live, oiled birds that are rehabilitated, does not begin to enumerate the impact of the spill on populations. It does not reveal the actual death toll, or the cost to birds in terms of their long-term ability to survive and reproduce. The complexities are numerous and lead to confusion when bird numbers are reported publicly."

Some believe that two years later, the spill has had worse results on nature than some expected or would admit. "Shrimp without eyes, crabs without claws and a fishing industry in decline - two years after the massive Gulf of Mexico oil spill, scientists and fishermen tell Al Jazeera that its impact is becoming clearer and things are getting worse"

"The rich ecosystems of Louisiana's marshlands have been damaged and are struggling to recover. And just one or two contaminated species can affect the entire food chain."

"Scott Eustis, a coastal wetlands specialist, says: 'We have some evidence of deformed shrimp, which is another developmental impact. So that shrimp's grandmother was exposed to oil while the mother was developing. But it's the grandchild of the shrimp that was exposed [that] grows up with no eyes.'"

"However, in a statement to Al Jazeera, BP says: 'Every seafood sample from reopened waters has undergone rigorous testing for oil and dispersants - and every sample from reopened waters has passed those tests.'"

"For the Gulf Coast's many fishermen the spill has had a dramatic effect. Half of all the oysters sold in the US used to come from Louisiana's waters but the region's fishermen now supply just one fifth," says Al Jazeera's inquiry into the spill in the spring of 2012.

Says Audubon Magazine, back in October 2010: "Comparing the count of dead birds that were collected with oil visible on their feathers from the Deepwater Horizon spill to the estimated toll from the Exxon Valdez oil spill is like comparing, well, apples to zebras. The 2,263 (Gulf of Mexico) birds collected dead with visible oil on their bodies is an actual count done, as all actual counts are done, imperfectly. The 225,000 from the Exxon Valdez is an estimate, calculated with a complex algorithm incorporating the death toll, numbers of oiled, live birds, and models and other estimates to create an educated, scientific guess about how many birds died." (Footnote six)

Finally, Michael volunteers what he thought emotionally of his experiences saving wildlife in this historic disaster inside the Gulf of Mexico. "How do you sum up one of the most amazing good and bad experiences of your life for the past two months in one sentence?" asks Michael. His most salient thought?

"It was the best time in my life, and at the same time, it was the worst time in my life: just witnessing the devastation. But, in having an impact, it was the experience of a lifetime to be down there involved in something like this. It is something that is going to be remembered and written about for decades to come. To be part of the rescue: It's something to tell my grandchildren about, if I ever have kids," he laughs.

Well, it wasn't the end of his work in the Gulf. Michael was sent back there in the winter season to protect wildlife while large clean up crews were picking up thousands more tar balls and sifting oil off the beaches.

Footnote one:
http://www.allaboutbirds.org/guide/Northern_Gannet/id
Footnote note two:
http://www.aqua.org/animals_diamondbackterrapin.html
Footnote three:
http://www.naturia.per.sg/buloh/birds/Egretta_alba.htm

Footnote four:
http://www.thedailygreen.com/environmental-news/latest/birds-gulf-oil-spill
Footnote five:
http://registremblay.wordpress.com/2010/11/02/the-bp-oil-spill
Footnote six: http://magblog.audubon.org/how-many-birds-died-bp-oil-spill

Some animals, based on their reputations, tend to scare or bother some of us, so we don't appreciate their comic antics. Bears can be comedians, as we see from the following tale.

The Black Bears Repeatedly Raid Bird Feeders

Three times during several summers, medium-sized black bears, attracted to my green metal-poled box or three hanging plastic tube bird feeders, descended upon our Litchfield, Connecticut, countryside back yard. Before I spotted two of these creatures, inaccurately viewed by many as necessarily dangerous to humans, I had heard all sorts of fascinating accounts of local sightings from others. Of course, those bears' distant relatives, especially the Grizzly and the Polar Bears, not the Brown Bear, are the ones with the real predator reputations, oft times unjustly rubbing off on Black Bears.

I had only observed Black Bears or their cubs myself as a boy or young man. I spotted them while exploring wooded areas and hiking mountains with my family in Eastern and Western Canada, or while hiking, fishing and camping in Northern Maine.

One appeared to have a desire to pop into one of our tents adjacent to Moose Head Lake. But, through our sudden movements and loud commands, we successfully chased him back into the forest. Another was eating wild blueberries on a Maine island inside on that very same lake, while we were picking them for breakfast pancakes.

Each time a Black Bear surprised me in the woods in vacation trips to Maine or Canada, my fear was almost overcome by fascination. A couple of times I sneaked up close enough with my Brownie Box Camera to snap a couple of photos of one of them. 'Ha,' I exclaimed to myself in my frightened mind, 'I can't wait to see these shots, and show them to everyone!'

Here is the best of the bear shots! I caught the beauty inside the lens before that black fuzzy one could scamper on. But, this shot was taken in my own Connecticut back yard more recently, not in northern Maine or Canada when I was just a boy. (Photo by Dennie Williams)

In reality though, these bears can be playful and funny. "Black bears use sounds, body language, and scent-marking to express their emotions of the moment…(they) not only communicate with grunts, tongue-clicks, and blowing. They have a resonant voice. It is not the barking, growling voice of a dog and is seldom the shrill voice of a house cat. It is distinctly bear-like with a near human quality that is easy to mimic," says The North American Bear Center.

That fascinating center's research tells this fascinating story: "On July 24, 2004, a (human's) baby cried while a parent changed its diapers at bedtime. Outside, a mother bear appeared and pressed her nose against a big picture window four feet away. She stood up with her paws against the glass, craning her neck to look and listen until the baby was quiet. She then walked off into the darkness with her cubs." The informational item did not say where this incident happened. (Footnote one)

Bears usually travel alone. The males, called Boars, are hostile to other males during the breeding season. Internet photos and videos show them attempting to climb on hammocks, struggling along airborne along a bird feeder lines or drinking beer. One big black one reportedly got drunk and passed out after allegedly drinking 36 cans of beer in Baker Lake, Washington. Don't believe me?! Check it out on kevinfreitas.net. (Footnote two)

I love the sight of playful looking, round, black bears and especially the cubs. However, a mother accompanying her cubs, occasionally can charge a human and attack. When humans are wary and careful, however, those incidents are rare. Bears' attacks turned out to be my younger days' fantasy, created by too many hyped nature adventure stories I heard or read. Over decades of occasional experiences, black bears always seemed more interested in our family picnic food, available either in our hands, tents, knapsacks or better yet, bags of garbage. They have moderate hearing and weak sight, but sharp smelling noses. Although normally shy, they often become curious when spotting humans.

Black bears' in-the-wild diets include grasses, nuts, berries, fruits, acorns, roots, sunflower seeds, ants, bees, deer, moose, carrion, and spawning salmon or other fish. The females weigh from 110 to 250 pounds, while males can weigh in as high as 450 pounds. It's the males who get the wanderlust. They look around the woods so they can mate with several females.

My home, off and on since boyhood, known as the 1776 Osborn House, has been tucked away a couple of miles south of that beautiful, historic Litchfield. It is right next to diminutive, sometimes bubbling, but mostly the smooth, shallow waters of Butternut Brook. Nearby are the huge Ripley Swamp and several neighborhood forests and wetlands. Those wetlands are one of the largest natural homes for birds, fish and mammals in Litchfield County.

Gradually, within the past decade or so, the forests around these wetlands and others in nearby White Memorial nature preserve have become more and more alluring for bears to create their habitats.

Bears love brooks, swamps and tree lines. In 2006 alone, The Litchfield Enquirer, the town's former weekly paper, noted 25 black bear sightings around town. A year earlier, the state reported black bears were most common in Litchfield County.

In June 2009 a state trooper shot a wandering bear to death after a hit-and-run SUV driver ran over it along Route 202, not far from my home.

A couple of months later, two big Black Bears, sighted further north in Goshen, created a lot of excitement among residents there.

A wandering 250-pound black bear further north in the center of Winsted was spotted by townspeople near a school. It was eventually tracked to its hiding place, a tree, and tranquilized by state foresters.

Officials say the black bear population has hit 900,000 throughout North America, says Bearsmart.com in 2012.

During our own first bear home visitation, I had returned to the house early on a summer evening from my 45-minute city workplace commute.

Soon after the car's engine silenced, I heard my wife, Ina, still holding a garden watering hose, exclaim: "There's a bear here! It was right here behind the flower garden! I was watering over there, and the bear popped up where I was spraying! I sprayed it! It's out there," she exclaimed, while gesturing toward the back yard lawn, adjacent to the brook.

Immediately, I walked out onto the lawn for a look. As I progressed, I heard repeated loud warnings from Ina: "Don't go there! It's still here!" I quickly looked in every direction along the small lawn, including at my untouched metal bird feeder. There was no bear in sight! It had disappeared across the brook and into hilly woodland nearby.

The bear had refused to leave, says Ina, even after she unknowingly sprayed it with the garden's watering hose, and it popped up near her home-grown flowers. It backed off a few feet, but then decided to look leisurely around the yard.

Ina says she rushed inside the house and retrieved two metal pot tops from the kitchen. She returned to the porch and from a safe distance, began banging them at the bear. It walked undeterred along the lawn toward a potential target, the metal bird feeder sitting on a four-foot metal pole.

However, its black hulk stopped short of the feeder. Instead, as the pot top banging continued, it retreated toward the brook at the end of the lawn. Undaunted, the fuzzy black fellow continued to hang around until I drove into the driveway, says Ina.

After anxiously and unsuccessfully exploring the lawn for signs of the bear, I quickly walked back to the exact spot where Ina first spotted it. There on the ground in front of me was my almost empty plastic tube bird feeder with the top stripped off. The bear had ripped it from the wire holding it to the big maple tree limb above. Strewn about the dead leaves and the dirt was most of the feeder's sunflower seed.

Later, Ina told me she was not afraid of the bear, just shocked and surprised by watering it with the hose. She knew her car was nearby, and she could retreat into it, so fear was not a factor, she says.

Well, we didn't see a bear for a couple of years or so after that encounter. However, in the meantime, we heard plenty of stories about bears from neighbors and friends.

One wandered into a female neighbor's garden. She took an excellent color photo of the bear walking inside her yard. That image appeared in a prime spot inside The Litchfield Enquirer, then the aged weekly newspaper and now deceased.

Still another bear, or maybe the same one, attacked a bird feeder belonging to a honey bee keeper near the town's wooded Prospect Mountain, a couple of miles from us. John Baker, the keeper, says he made sure afterward to take down his bird feeder before going to bed every evening, and created protections for his bee hives, still untouched by the furry black fellow.

The next bear appeared in our own yard, many months later. That male bear, appearing to weigh about 250 pounds, pawed the bird feeder's four-foot metal pole to the ground. The beast ripped the green metal feeder off of it, opened its top and began eating birdseed to his heart's content. Ina caught sight of the bear first and warned me where it was feasting. I spotted the green box feeder on the ground next to a laying bear pawing and eating seed freely. Ina immediately telephoned a State Department of Environmental Protection official to find out the best course of action. The official asked her if the bear had a red ear tag. When she said, "Yes," he wanted to know the number on it.

Incredulous, Ina told him she would never want to get close enough to read the tag. To trace its travels, a state park official, after shooting a sleeping potion into it, had stapled the tag to the stun-gunned beast as he had done with many other bears.

Ina had never been enthusiastic about my constant purchases of fifteen to twenty dollar 40 and 50 pound sunflower seed bags. She became elated when the DEP official told her one way to discourage bears' backyard visits is not to feed the birds until November, after the bears hibernate.

Enthusiastically, the day of the bear's visit, Ina rushed outside, after the beast was long gone, and handed me the phone with the DEP official waiting on the other end of the line. She told me that official had a big Black Bear-message for me. "Don't feed the birds until November," he told me, "because that's when the bears hibernate."

Sarcastically, I asked him, "Is it unhealthy to feed the birds sunflower seeds in summer?" When he replied, "No," I told him: "Sir, you don't know me! I have always been friendlier to bears than people!" He replied with apparent surprise, "Oh," and then quickly exited the phone with a hasty good-bye.

Our next bear visit occurred later in the summer. It was then I discovered, to my horror that my green box metal bird feeder was no longer standing.

I glanced around frantically. There, not far from the bent pole holding it, I saw a big bear once again lying next to the green box on the lawn and pawing sunflower seeds into his mouth. At first, I began screaming at it, but almost immediately I realized that I first wanted a photo. My camera happened to be nearby on the porch. I focused the lens in from afar. However, one glance at the image revealed the bear was too far away, and in the late afternoon, the scene was too dark.

Having heard my earlier screams, Tommie, our adult son, rushed outside the house, took the camera from me and began stalking the bear for the best of shots. It became a funny, short adventure.

Neither of us had intimidated the bear. It was reluctant to leave a potential birdseed feast. The big fellow actually seemed a bit curious about the two of us as we stalked it from 20 or more yards away.

Soon, the furry one dropped down and waddled off in a rush toward the nearby brook as if to fake a jump into it. But, instead, it veered back in the opposite direction in a diagonal, straight toward the vicinity of one of the plastic tube bird feeders ripped down previously by the other bear.

It stopped suddenly next to a large Maple tree and immediately looked like it was ready to climb. Instead, the big fellow raised up again on hind legs, put one paw against the tree and stared at us while showing off his chest. Its rounded ears stood straight up. Its brownish snout, with no teeth showing, was pointed right at us. His big, glaring brown eyes and curved mouth made him look mischievous, not scary.

Bears sometimes claw and rub their smell onto a tree to mark it territorially, but that was not happening. It felt like the bear was actually amused by us. But, as we stood staring at that standing, glaring bear, my fear of bears took over again. Wow! I couldn't believe how much larger the black fellow looked on its hind feet! It seemed a bit taller than Tommie who is over 6 feet 2 inches tall. It made me hesitant to continue the chase.

The bear appeared to be saying: "Hey, I can climb this big tree if need be! Or, I can handle you guys, because look how big and tall I am!"

As I stayed put on the lawn. Tommie moved closer with the camera at the ready. Thinking Tommie already had too many photos of a dark bear in dim light, I screamed and feigned a move in the bear's direction. He dropped down and fled with a curious me running after him, but safely behind him. It was amazing how fast the rotund bear with round limbs vibrating through black fur disappeared into the underbrush in the direction of the brook. I later learned they can run as fast as 35 miles per hour!

The whole experience was fitting in spirit for this section of Robert Frost's poem, "The Bear."

"The bear puts both arms around the tree above her
And draws it down as it were a lover

And its chokecherries lips to kiss good-by.

Then lets it snap back upright in the sky,

Her next step rocks a bolder on the wall

(She's making her cross-country in the fall).

Her great weight cracks the barbed wire in its staples
As she flings over and off through the maples,
Leaving on one wire tooth a lock of hair." (Footnote three)

Sometimes bears react to scared or aggressive people with their own brand of hostility, like a running charge in the direction of the annoying human. Of course, with a Grizzly, that could ultimately be fatal for anyone. Indeed, even two Grizzly bears' friends, Tim Treadwell and Annie Huguenard, studying and photographing them in Alaska in October 2003, were unexpectedly attacked and tragically killed by one of the big beasts. Treadwell went out to meet it, but the bear attacked him, and as that was going on warned Huguenard inside a tent. The whole episode was recorded in six minutes of camera film. The camera was strangely flicked on by Huguenard before the bear attacked her too. (Footnote four)

Footnote one:

www.bear.org/website/index.php?option=com_cont ent&view=article&id=66:the-black-bears-voice&catid=16&Itemid=42

Footnote two:
http://www.kevingfrietas.net/journal/beer-drinking-bear/

Footnote three: The Poetry of Robert Frost (Paperback) By Robert Frost, Edward Connery Lathem http:www.poemhunter.com/poem/the-bear/

Footnote four:
http://deathaday.blogspot.com/2007/10/grizzly-timothy-treadwell-and-amie.html

But, while bears can attack, other creatures, like birds and squirrels, have their own means of startling, perplexing and haunting humans who annoy them. My closest boyhood friend, Barney Burrall, otherwise known as BBB, tells his own funny story next.

But before that tale, Grey Squirrel creatures are defined!

The Squirrel Roams

Many grey or red squirrel watchers can easily hatch descriptions of how the nutty creatures roam, eat, play, and occasionally stay home with the kids.

Squirrels! Squirrels! Squirrels! Aptly Named! Cheeek…Cheeek…Cheeek, the grey ones screech when inspired or just when they feel like it. The little red squirrels have a shorter but more repetitious Chik, Chik, Chik call. They are not as frequently seen as the greys, and usually travel alone.

The greys are silver-grey in summer and browner grey in winter, and when mature grow to a foot in length generally with a sleek body, and always with a curled, fluffy, round tail.

Routinely, when moving out above, they jump from bough to bough in almost every tree immediately available. They too, like those slow moving, much bigger ground hogs, can rest, but their temporary couches are normally atop tree limbs, not in open fields or underground.

On the turf, Grey Squirrels with their white breasts speed as fast as a line of water from a hose's tightest nozzle. They often chase one another in zig-zags across lawns and fields, and even up tree trunks.

Once the chaser catches the target on the open ground, the two enjoy rolling around momentarily in the leaves or the dirt.

While up in the trees, they just keep up the race flying from bough to bough, usually without an ending struggle.

Typically, Grey Squirrels, ending their tree work, or play or rest periods, pick a low spot from which to drop to the ground landing face first on their front haunch. They can then move out on all four feet as if shot out of a gun. They stop on a dime. They stand up on their two back legs showing their fluffy white breasts and usually look all around their 180-degree parameter.

Some can stay in a still alert post like that, as if hypnotized, for minutes at a time. Others drop to all fours within seconds of their stand ups and rove on with little hops to their target destination. They do that either all at once, or with seconds-worth of multiple stops on all fours along the way.

Of course, their prime ground destination is almost always a spot where nuts, fruits, fungi, lichens, buds, mushrooms, roots, pine cones, leaves, twigs and bark are likely to lie, says BBI Squirrel World. Sometimes they eat standing on their back wheels. Oft times, they either tuck a nut in their cheek for travel or dig a hole nearby for storage.

If chased by man or beast, they speed to the nearest tree, grab the bark with claws, circle around and around and up its trunk, jump bough to bough, moving from one nearby tree to another until they seemingly disappear into space elsewhere.

They do like to nest particularly at night in a round chamber of twigs and attached leaves or nestled ones bigger than a basketball, and typically located high in a tree.

Country Grey Squirrels, unlike city dwellers regularly fed by park visitors, are not prone to being tame with people. They can seem curious if they sense a person looks or acts friendly. Then, they hang low on the bottom of a tree's base or a low branch and stare with seeming curiosity.

Many are wary perhaps because they have been chased from bird feeders or screamed at or attacked by angry bird-lovers. Only in the city, after being used to scores of friendly people feeding them, do squirrels become human-sociable by sitting and eating just feet away.

Sometimes Grey Squirrels' brazen activities gain them national publicity. In two amusing episodes, a squirrel or two invaded the St. Louis Cardinals' Busch Stadium during two October 2011 crucial National League playoff games. The squirrel or squirrels created a stir by racing across the field in the midst the two playoffs between the Cardinals and the Philadelphia Phillies.

The second appearance was most spectacular because the little grey racer flew across home plate just after the Phillies' pitcher delivered his pitch to a Cardinal's batter. The pitcher demanded a replay his pitch claiming he threw it off the plate as a result of squirrel speeding. But the claim was rejected by the umpire as a video showed the little guy cross the plate after the pitch was delivered.

Here's that very riveting scene from Skip Schumaker's baseball card created by Topps Baseball Cards. Better yet! Check out the video on Yahoo and YouTube! It cannot be missed! (Footnote one)

The batter said he never saw the squirrel even after it almost ran across his feet, but a lot of the crowd sure did. They scattered as the little beast ran into the stands near them. (Footnote two)

During an earlier game the same week, the first visitor squirrel disrupted players on the field and fans in the stands when darted across the infield, and then, after seeing thousands checking him out, fled under an outfield wall. (Footnote two)

This is a truly funny footnote! Skip Schumaker's baseball card for the following year (2012) doesn't show Skip! It shows the squirrel running across home plate near his foot! (Footnote three) Funnier yet, the Internet reveals that in February 2012, this baseball card sold for $600 on eBay. (Footnote four)

Footnote one:
http://sports.yahoo.com/mlb/blog/big_league_stew/post/squirrel-returns-to-busch-heads-for-home-during-at-bat?urn=mlb,wp22794

The YouTube video of the squirrel rushing across home plate:
http://www.youtube.com/watch?v=EsQYS5zS5u4

Footnote two:
http://www.stltoday.com/news/local/metro/article_7e74b1bc-a7bd-5a62-87c8-f8329b060253.html
Footnote three: http://sports.yahoo.com/blogs/mlb-big-league-stew/skip-schumaker-baseball-card-features-rally-squirrel-not-190252048.html
Footnote four:
http://offthebench.nbcsports.com/2012/02/02/skip-schumaker-rally-squirrel-topps-card-sells-for-600-on-ebay/

The Great White Squirrel Hunter As Yarned By Barnum Beach Burrall

Nicknamed Barney, I grew up in the Litchfield Hills in Connecticut. The year was 1954. I was 13. For my birthday, my father had given me his 22-caliber rifle that his father had given him at exactly the same age. Having read books about Davy Crockett and Daniel Boone, I knew how to dress for the woods: rubber boots, fitting just below the knees, jeans stuffed into the boots, and rawhide shirt topped off with a stunning coonskin hat complete with the animal's tail. My mother could hardly control the urge to burst out laughing, but managed to keep it together.

Our house set up presented me with the entire second floor as a bedroom. From my window I had a clear view some 200 feet across the back yard to four or five old apple trees. Thinking of myself as a great, white hunter while gazing out an open bedroom window, I would watch the squirrels climb and run around in the branches, and then stop for a snack. With careful slingshot aim, I became excellent at hitting them. After a successful hit, I would walk outside with my hunting knife and down to the carcass to cut off the tail, much like the Native Americans did to the heads of their enemies. Displaying a squirrel's tail seemed like the best way to show off my trophy to friends without experiencing the mess of skinning the hide.

Earlier, while I was way up there gazing down from the second floor window with slingshot at the ready, the experience felt more like firing at targets in a shooting gallery than killing live animals.

Behind our house was one thousand acres of woods, and those repetitious ancient story instructions from Davy and Daniel had well prepared me for my first adventure. After all, my friend, Dennie Williams, and I, using fake cap guns and bows and arrows, had played cowboys and Indians for years.

Now with my big-boy Beebe rifle and a clothing outfit that made me look like a cross between an adventurous buffalo hunting Teddy Roosevelt, and Ernest Hemingway, out for game in Africa, I was ready for action.

I knew I was supposed to sneak quietly through the forest so the big game wouldn't hear me. But, those damn boots kept catching on fallen branches and tree roots and revealing my whereabouts. So I gave up on my idea of sneaking around and clomped along, letting everything, seemingly within a mile, hear me coming. I carried my weapon with both hands until I cramped up. Then, casually, I shifted it to my right hand. All the while, I had no expectation for a serious ambush.

I had walked what seemed like miles when I came to a babbling brook. There I noticed rustling noise from a sudden movement in the trees above me. Gazing up, I saw a menacing squirrel now sitting on a branch annoyed and incessantly chattering at me.

I placed the gun barrel upwards at the ready. With anxious aim, I pulled the trigger and watched closely as the squirrel tumbled to the ground, immediately regained its feet and ran into a nearby ground hole.

As any brave hunter knows, you need to instantaneously chase down your prey and bring home the bacon. I ran over to the hole. There, staring up at me from a shallow hole was a very angry, chattering rodent. Because I wasn't experienced in this kind of situation, I reached into the hole and tried to grab the critter. I did so because I was prepared to use my other weapon, a ten-inch Bowie knife that hung heavily from my belt.

I suppose in my imagination that day that I thought I would stab this screeching varmint and cook it for lunch.

What happened next influenced my hunting career forever. The little bugger tried to bite me. I pulled my hand out of the hole in a flash! That did it! My immediate panicked thought: Neither my imagined namesake Daniel Boone nor I was going to die in that forest from a rabies infested squirrel bite.

It had seemed like hours walking thought brush to finally reach that stream. It felt a whole lot shorter getting back home. On the way back, I couldn't help but think how casually I regularly dispatched those squirrels, sitting nearby in the apple trees, as I sling-shotted at them from my upstairs bedroom window.

After my face-to-face encounter in the woods, I somehow had a whole new perspective. Yes, that squirrel was hostile, but wouldn't I have been too if I was up in a tree, fired upon, knocked to the ground, and pursued by hostile human's hand into a hole in the ground?

Really, I thought, here was an innocent animal, minding its own business, trying to survive, while an obviously rookie hunter was trying to shoot it to death, just to cut off its tail and show it off to friends.

I ventured out many times into forests anticipating childhood nature adventures after that day, but had lost my Daniel Boone swagger and my taste for killing squirrels.

Instead of hunting squirrels, Barney decided gardening was more exciting. (Photographer Unidentified)

Squirrels, The Acrobats, The Raiders, The Flying Invaders

In the old days when Barney and I were childhood friends, I had an ever-present desire to punish Grey Squirrels, without killing them. But my motivation had nothing whatsoever to do with imagining myself as a great white hunter.

To me, squirrels were constant pests. Most of my life, I have routinely fed the birds next to my homes with sunflower seeds and suet, stored in feeders of all kinds: plastic tubes, metal boxes or metal screens, used for animal fat. Almost every week, squirrels invaded those feeders no matter how I fortified or protected them. They jumped from trees or the roofs of houses. Sometimes they even jumped up to cling to whatever hung down. At other times, they type-roped along thin wires, holding feeder boxes. I frequently was awakened by vague, but horrifying nightmares sparked by their thin light grey bodies and fluffy tails flying through the air!

I still remember being awakened in my room inside our ancient, historical salt box home on Brush Hill Road, Litchfield, by the loud squirrel scratching noises from a bird feeder attached to my window sill. In those days, I had purchased a Beebe gun to fire at what I then considered "those little beasts." I never used it for much else except routine target shooting, or pretend-cowboy missions into the woods or corn fields. Fortunately, I was not a good shot. If I ever hit a squirrel, it simply fell harmlessly to the ground and scurried away. Sometimes when hit by my Beebe shot, it simply leaped off a limb to another tree branch.

Other times, I unsuccessfully fought the Grey Squirrels off with my throat clearing screams, or with flying rocks or snowballs. I was so obsessed that I even created little piles of ammunition, palm-sized rocks and fist-sized snowballs. I stored them outside my homes' doors, not far from my bird feeders.

Not long after I married my beautiful German wife, Ina, in 1970, we moved up the road a stone's throw from my old home to a log cabin in the woods. We brought up two children, our daughter, Gisela, and son, Tommie, who is three years younger than his sister.

When he was a young boy, Tommie frequently listened with hidden annoyance to my daily squirrel screams. He then watched me rush out of the cabin to grab the rocks or snow balls to toss at those bird feeder-invaders. I didn't realize for a long while that he was silently angry at what he considered Dad's senseless behavior toward innocent critters.

Finally, one day, when Tommie, was a middle schooler, he nailed an unprotected wooden shelf to a pine tree right next to the house, and filled it with birdseed. I couldn't believe what I saw the moment I walked outside!

As I quickly glanced back at the house in disbelief, I spotted Tommie gazing with amusement out a large sliding glass door. Seconds after spotting his peering eyes, I rushed back inside the door to confront him.

"Did you do that?! Did you nail that shelf to the pine tree?!" I asked in frustrated disbelief.

"Dad! Yes, I did that! You are so stupid!" Before storming off into another room, Tommie told me he was sick of seeing me attack squirrels. He exclaimed: "They deserve to live too, Dad!"

Believe it or not, that was close to the end of my squirrel attacking days, which had begun most probably at an age even younger than Tommie. It took a day or so before Tommie's words sunk in, and when they did, I actually became embarrassed about the apparent bitter dislike I had for such a beautiful and lively creature.

Bird and nature lovers I knew chuckled when I repeatedly spun my squirrel-battling tales.

One day, when I was visiting a neighborhood party, I ran into a friend of the family's - especially a buddy of my father's. Thomas Witherspoon and I soon began trading our tales of countless annoying squirrels' bird feeder invasions.

Tom told me he too had long standing battles with squirrels burglarizing his own yard's bird feeder. But, he said, ultimately, he discovered a "fantastic" homemade squirrel prevention device. He simply "hot wired" his bird feeder to an electrical switch inside his house, so he could flick it on, and instantaneously electrify the feeder upon a squirrel's arrival. The electrical charge was not strong enough to harm the squirrel, but it "sure as heck shocked the bugger off the feeder," he exclaimed with a broad smile.

This tale was so inspiring, I quickly passed it on to a friend of mine, Steve Grant, The Hartford Courant's nature writer. He was interested! In fact, said Steve, he was just drafting a feature story on the various means bird lovers utilize to prevent squirrels from barging onto feeders. He asked me for Mr. Witherspoon's contact information to interview him. Some weeks afterward, his story, hit the Courant's front page! It sure was entertaining reading!

I got to thinking about Steve and his story not long afterward, when Ina and I were taking a break up in Woodstock, Vermont. I walked into a local bookstore and spotted a beautiful post card of a Grey Squirrel climbing a tree. A mischievous idea struck me immediately! It compelled me to write Steve a wild and critical note about his story on this beautiful squirrel post card. But, before I could do so, an even greater coincidence occurred.

I was reading the Sunday Hartford Courant's comic section when I spotted a small cartoon box. It depicted two Grey Squirrels sitting on a bird feeder, eating their hearts out and chatting. One squirrel was telling the other:

"Boy is this bird seed delicious!"

The other replied:

"Yes and just wait till that bird lover sees us!"

So I glued that diminutive cartoon onto the back of the squirrel post card and wrote this: "Dear Mr. Grant, Alleged Nature Writer, You should be ashamed of yourself! What are you doing suggesting all sorts of ways to attack us in your recent news story? Remember?! We are squirrels, members of the wild nature community, which you are always suggesting should be protected at all costs! You, Mr. Grant, need to be more careful what you write! Most Sincerely, A squirrels' union representative"

I then drove to the post office, bought a stamp and asked a male clerk an odd question. "Is it possible for me to stamp this card myself with your official dating device and deliver it in person?" The clerk looked at me quizzically and replied, "No, sir that cannot be done!" But surprisingly, he then scanned my disappointed face and said, "I have this other, unofficial ink stamp you could use." He handed it to me. I pounded it onto the stamp on my own, and left with the card immediately to deliver it via Dennie-post.

Upon arrival at The Courant, I became elated! I figured a plan! The newsroom on the second floor had a huge, walled shelf of open, accessible mailboxes. So I found the one marked Steve Grant, and special-delivered the card to that mailbox. Then, I asked a nearby news clerk whether Steve had arrived yet, and, as it turned out, he hadn't. But, I knew he was mostly on time for work starting at 10 a.m. It was just minutes before the hour. So I hid myself in a spot where I could see both the mailboxes and his desk further into the large newsroom. Sure enough, Steve soon arrived, gathered his mail and walked to his desk.

Fortunately, Steve looked at his mail immediately upon arrival. Soon, even from far across the room, I could see the startled look on his face. He was obviously in the midst of reading the squirrel's post card. Then, even better, he summoned a couple of other reporters over to his desk. They soon all started pointing and laughing hilariously at the card.

I am estimating, but I would say that some days, or a week later, I walked by Steve's desk, and remarked casually, but with a telling smile: "Hey, Steve, have you received much of a reaction to your squirrel story?" He looked up and almost immediately exclaimed: "Oh, now I know! It was you that sent that card!" I tried to deny it, but my loud, boisterous laughter gave me away.

I must admit that I, like my boyhood friend, Barney, I hunted once, but not just for squirrels. It was only a single occasion, but confessions are necessary for one preaching love and communications with wild animals and birds. The hunt was experienced in another country, South Korea, while I was a lieutenant in the U.S. Army.

The One Time Haunting Korean Hunt

I never expected that I would ever wield a shotgun and track down game. But, I did not get in a hunter's mood overnight. Hunting was a once in a lifetime experience when I was in my early twenties, and susceptible to hunters' influences. I have never liked weapons of any kind, and still don't. I am passionately in opposition to The National Rifle Association and all pro-gun groups, except perhaps, Ducks Unlimited because a part of their basic mission supports nature and conservation.

During the 1960s, the days of the draft and the Vietnam War, just after I finished working as an admissions interviewer of students at Middlebury College, I enlisted in the U.S. Army. Had it not been for the draft, I would never have joined the Army. I was incredibly anti-military, but not then an actual peace-nick. I simply abhor the thought of violence, or anyone being armed with rifles, handguns or any other weaponry.

That distaste was strong enough in college that I may have been the only student in my class to flunk out of the Army Reserve Officer Training Corps. As a result, I was forced to go through basic training at Ft. Dix, New Jersey, an experience I truly never relished. There were regular hard-hated, green fatigue training sessions. We crawled on the ground with M-1 rifles, bayonets attached. The young recruits were taught to yell: "Kill, kill, kill!" as we crawled.

Once back in the barracks, training sergeants constantly harassed us, and yelled in our ears as we stood at full, straight up attention. I got through it, however. Then, because I did not want to be a private in the Army, I applied for officer artillery training at Ft. Sill, Oklahoma. Before finally graduating from that rigorous course, I flunked out as a lower class man. I was so ashamed. I was the only unsuccessful candidate in my class who recycled back into the program. Ultimately, I pressed myself through lower, middle and upper classes to become a second lieutenant. What a miracle it was to me then and even thinking about it today!

Part of that training aimed at making me an artillery forward observer to direct 105 Howitzer fire on far away enemy targets. As part of the training, the experienced artillerymen rushed the inexperienced out to a huge field in a speeding bus.

Once there, we were harassed outside to scan imaginary targets, and make an estimate of what our location instructions should be. I still remember vividly a day when I was ordered to run out of a bus into a forward observer post and rush-tested for direct fire on an imaginary target. My first screamed coordinates resulted in a howitzer round explosion just missing a far away barn, outside the target area.

Oh my gosh, was I scared! By some miracle, my very next instructions veered the howitzer shell within 50 yards of the target. What a lucky shot!

That and other nasty experiences made me determined to stay away from such activity, so I successfully applied to counterintelligence officer school in Baltimore, Maryland. There I was forced into tense interviews of actors and actresses, posing as difficult sources of information, and constantly attempting to embarrass me on stage in front of my class. Later, I trained out on the streets of the city to secretly tail or surveil, actors posing as elusive security violators or spies. In teams of three, we were ordered to follow an actor on the streets of the city.

Teams of three were spread out all over the city, each following one of these mischievous actors. One day, those actors all plotted to have coffee in the smallest coffee shop in Baltimore. As a result, our teams were swarming like bees and bumping into one another and innocent pedestrians, all around the outside of that shop. Our targets must have laughed themselves silly if they looked out of the coffee shop's window.

After this intensive training, I was assigned in 1964 for a year's tour with the 191st Military Intelligence Detachment in Paju-Ri, South Korea, very close to the North Korean border. There I soon made close friendships with the five Korean interpreters the unit intensely utilized to interrogate North Korean border-crossers. One of them, nicknamed Charlie O, was a determined hunter of ducks, pheasants, small water deer and wild boars.

Constantly, Charlie O spun hunting stories. He exhorted all of his friends and colleagues to take trips into territories where we could pursue his favorite game. I told him I had never hunted any game except, I joked, squirrels with a Beebe gun.

Charlie O kept after me to go hunting, particularly when I posed with another interpreter, Mr. Kim, for a photo of me holding a small North Korean machine gun confiscated from a border crosser by South Korean military intelligence. Because I was beginning to feel like 'a chicken,' and wanted to please a good friend, I ultimately agreed I would hunt with him. My only arms-training ever had been the use of the Army's M-1 rifle, soon after I enlisted a couple of years earlier.

Immediately below is an amended version of the letter I wrote my mother and father on March 7, 1965, about Charlie O's hunting adventure. If it sounds a bit macho, I was only 24 or 25 years old then.

Today if I accidentally ran down a squirrel or any other animal or bird with my car, I would experience a serious guilt trip. I could never, ever hunt, period! But, I need to be transparent and honest with all you readers. In this book I present myself as a nature lover, and a rare human being who learned to interact and communicate with animals and birds.

This is a confession of what I now consider a one-time sin, before I was such an intense believer in the world of the wild creatures. On the other hand, this belief by no means detracts from the respect I have for befriended, experienced and responsible hunters. Charlie O is one of those I will never, ever forget!

With appropriate editing and some needed additions, here is the letter I sent to my parents:

Yesterday Charlie 0, the notorious huntsman of the 191st drove us into the 25th Republic of Korea Army sector on a stalking trip. We left our detachment about nine o'clock in the morning and arrived in our jeep in the area about an hour later. Coordinating with our ROK Army counterparts North East of our own compound, they assigned a Counterintelligence Corps ROK Army guide and an old Korean hunter-guide with his small trained and clever mongrel dog.

I was impressed that they worried so much about our safety, because, as I was later to find out, there were a lot of old landmines in the area. Had we stepped on one, and detonated it, more than one of us could have been killed or seriously wounded.

Charlie O invited an old hunting associate who had explored this particular northern area next to the Demilitarized Zone between South and North Korea quite a few times. That low mountain vicinity contains several small valleys, quite comfortable for uphill hunt-strolling. It is filled with rice paddies, low brushes and high, dry grasses.

Before we got underway, there was a constant echoing sound from a strong, seemingly far away, powerful microphone. At first, the sound seemed hauntingly blurred, but apparently a North Korean technician or our change in location corrected it. Then, at least I, being new to this particular area, very close to the 38th Parallel or North Korean border, was shocked not by a foreign, but an American soldier's voice. That vocalization expressed repeatedly something like: 'Hello, I was a U.S. Army soldier. I defected to North Korea. It's wonderful here. Come on over and visit Shangri-La!'

I know that several U.S. Army soldiers had defected in the 1960s, but I had no idea any of them had become propaganda microphone voices like this. It was shocking and pathetic. South Korean intelligence reports express what a depressing, closed and confined world U.S. Army soldier defectors to North Korea live in.

As the echoes reverberated again and again, I tried to ignore them. Eventually, as hunting action took over my consciousness, I heard only the echoing sounds, and paid no heed to the words.

Our wild creature stalking crew of over a half dozen split into varying groups, exploring neighboring shrubby areas, containing small, thin trees among the modest hills and narrow valleys. We all started out with speed, enthusiasm and the promise of adventure.

The busy, roving dog soon flushed three pheasants out of a riverbed. Being the novice, I didn't have the chance to shoot. The experienced Korean hunters took three shots, all of which missed their marks.

We then moved through this first marshy area rather quickly. The thirst for game intensified through that initial sighting of pheasants. As we were just leaving a second tree-filled hunting neighborhood in vain, we noticed that Papa San's energetic dog was circling in on an object of interest inside a thicket. We waited and listened closely for a few minutes. Then, impatiently and expectantly, we began sweeping the dog's targeted area, as he continued to circle and bark.

Within seconds, I walked directly forward, and a pheasant scampered, then flew right out from beneath brush just yards my feet. The bright feathered one seemed so fast, and I was so inexperienced that it was gone from my vision before I knew it. Charlie 0 and the others in the party spotted its silhouette hit the sky. Three of them shot and missed, but Charlie, with his keen eye and immaculate sense of timing, brought it down.

The old mongrel dog, a rather shaggy, common likeable type, immediately ran off to the spot of the bird's crash landing. I was later told he waited, standing patiently over the struggling bird, until his master, the Papa San, could get to the scene. As Papa San had rushed off, I called after him to bring the bird back for a look. Soon, he appeared and handed me the pheasant to hold. I was startled. The bird was still alive in my hands!

Charlie had wounded it in the wing. Before I had a chance to call the Association for the Protection of Animals (joke), Charlie strolled over, took it from my hand, broke its neck over his shotgun barrel, and strapped it under the Papa San's belt.

This was my quick, shocking initiation to Korean hunting!

Shortly thereafter, we embarked on one of the longest and most leg-tiring sweep of any countryside that I, in my short life, have ever undertaken. We rushed up long rice paddy valleys, climbed through and up other little valleys indented in the mountains, and made our way through marshy areas fighting through thickets of long straw-colored marsh weeds. This furious hunting initiation was driving me into the ground. I slowed down a bit in a sweat, as the others continued on in a rush.

The echoing North Korean microphone propaganda, using the U.S. defected servicemen continued. Before I knew it, I heard many repetitious shotgun shots from up in a valley. I moved around in my position on a hill to get a better look at what was going on, but trees and shrubs blocked the view.

Suddenly, looking through a gap in the bushes, I spotted a Sika Deer running a full speed down the valley below, and jumping from higher-level rice paddies to lower level ones. It took me a while to react, as the sight stunned me. While the deer was running on a diagonal toward, but well below me, I started to run down the side of the mountain to cut the little one off. I ran into and around continual natural barriers like rocks trees, shrubs and briars on the way down. So I could not concentrate on viewing the deer's changing whereabouts.

By the time I had made it to the hill's very bottom, my legs were whipped to death by small clinging vines and briars along the path; my breath was wagging a war on my lungs; and the deer was "opso," or gone. This chase freshened my appetite for the hunt, even though while thinking about it, I was sure I didn't have the heart or the ability to shoot such a speedy little creature.

Within some minutes, I rejoined most of the hunting crew who had by this time bagged themselves four or five birds. They had finished sweeping one side of the valley, and were starting on the other side when I rejoined them.

While making our way up one of the many indents in the mountain (valley-lets), our energetic dog began his frequent excited barking, smelling, rushing and circling. Papa San knew right away that Bess, as he called her, was just about to flush another bird.

We all stopped and waited with our weapons poised for the kill. I heard wings flapping about 25 yards in front of me. In a flash, I caught sight of an airborne pheasant. Pointing my shotgun in the general direction, I pulled tight on the trigger. The noise echoed hurtfully in my ears, while the shotgun's vibration jolted my right shoulder. Papa San fired simultaneously.

The bird dropped to the ground. I couldn't really tell whose shot hit it. Right then, while I was still reeling from my shotgun's blast, I suspected Papa San had been on target, not me.

Before I could say a word he looked right at me and exclaimed: "You number one shot! You number one shot!" He was so insistent that I could only keep quiet and accept his praise!

Papa San knew what he was doing in the bush. I didn't. Charlie O approached with the dead pheasant in hand. While smiling broadly, he soon dodged around me and strapped it to the back of my pants. Just as Charlie was doing that, Papa San drew blood from the pheasant onto his fingers. He took hold of my lower right arm and wiped the pheasant's blood on my wrist. That was the sign, he said, that I was now a true hunter.

From then on, I was considered part of the Korean club of those successful hunters, even if, in my own mind, my shot was a dubious one. But I went along with Papa San's version. What did I know?! From that point onward, I convinced myself to swagger and strut a bit through the bushes. It began to seem like my energy increased to the point that my legs knew no hill's barrier too steep or no hunting path too long.

Shortly thereafter, we finished the first part of the hunt, and went back to base camp, our starting point, to count our game and eat the Army rations that Charlie and I had brought.

Once collected in a group, we noticed that Charlie's friend, Mr. Yi, was missing. Within a short time, however, we heard a succession of shots, a pause and another series of shots.

About a half hour later, while we were eating our meal, Mr. Yi arrived, holding a badger hanging by its hind feet. A shotgun was slung his free arm, and two pheasants strapped to his belt. We congratulated him, looked over briefly to verbally admire his badger, and soon resumed lunch.

That afternoon we swept other areas for game with little success. I missed while firing a single shot at another pheasant.

Not long afterward, Mr. Yi, working the opposite side of the hill from me, fired three fast shots. By the time I joined him, a deer was in its death throws in the grass. Bess, Papa San's dog, smelled the fresh blood and rushed in for the kill, but the old man, uttering fierce orders and reprimands, miraculously stopped him in his paw tracks. After all had glanced at the animal, Mr. Yi carried it back to the road. He covered it with weeds so that he could continue the hunt.

On the sweeps that followed, my hunting colleagues bagged a few more pheasants, an anticlimax to Mr. Yi's earlier effort. The chase's momentum slowed. Papa San insisted we had exhausted the available game in the area, so we all threw our weapons over our shoulders and ended the hunt.

Top shows Charlie O, (left) and Dennie readying for the hunt. Middle depicts the guide and his dog to the left of the picture and two hunters to the right. The bottom again reveals the hunting guide who initiated Dennie with the blood of a freshly killed pheasant. (Photos By Dennie Williams)

That night Charlie O, Mr. Yi, Captain Kim, who had arranged the hunt, and assorted other Korean men, unknown to me, celebrated the morning's and afternoon's hunting festivities in a Ginseng House with plenty to eat and drink.

The people living in the restaurant-bar's small village all crowded around our parked Jeep in amazement at the game inside it. Every once in a while, one of us left the party to check and see that all our game was still there.

To Koreans, game is necessary food, not an opportunity to show off a trophy. No question! All of it was not to be wasted. These hunters would not even think of such a thing!

Well I hope that Ma is not alarmed by my frank description of the hunt, or by my initiation as a hunter. The sport certainly is refreshing, particularly after being cooped up in a military compound for a while, I concluded at the end of my letter.

Hunters! Check It Out And Think About It: Being a Vegan Makes Sense For Humans and Grizzlies Alike

Responsible hunters, too, enjoy and love animals, and in fact, some hunters, because they are regularly out in the wild, often have a greater appreciation and knowledge of wildlife than those without constant exposure to nature.

American Indians hunted Bison, but they did so to feed themselves or use the skins of animals for clothing. They mostly killed with restraint and respect for their prey. Their experiences in the wild gave them great admiration for the animal, the bird and the fish. It is legend that when the Buffalo began to die off and become sparse, tribes living alongside them lost much of their zest and enthusiasm for living.

"The American Indian lived a life being one with nature. In their way, they understood the ecological demands of the land and knew that if they took care of the land the land would take care of them. They possessed an untouched wisdom living in harmony with the environment. They hunted the land for buffalo, which provided food and clothing for the ages to come. In time they would almost become non existent at the hands of the 'white' man. They would come to lose their land, lose the buffalo and lose their self being and their way of life," says The American Treatment Of The Indian Tribes. (Footnote one)

Whether it is a hunter or a close observer of nature, the key to loving and appreciating wild creatures arises from spontaneous or unexpected joyful encounters with them.

The true spirited hunter goes out into the forest with utter respect for the environs and his quarry, making sure he hunts only allowable game and ultimately uses it for food. If a hunter wounds a fleeing animal or bird, he or she is ethically required to chase it down and finish the mission.

Here is the philosophy I learned through conversations with those I knew to be nature lovers, yet hunters too!

"The hunter pursues animals because he loves them and sympathizes with them, and kills them as the champions of chivalry used to slay one another — courteously, fairly, and with admiration and respect. To stalk and shoot the elk and the grizzly bear is to him what wooing and winning a beloved maiden would be to another man. Far from being the foe or exterminator of the game he follows, he, more than any one else, is their friend, vindicator, and confidant. A strange mutual ardor and understanding unites him with his quarry. He loves the mountain sheep and the antelope, because they can escape him; the panther and the bear, because they can destroy him. His relations with them are clean, generous, and manly." From "American Wild Animals in Art," non-fiction book by Julian Hawthorne.

This was a philosophy I knew about before that day of the hunt near the borders of South and North Korea. Indeed, it is a spirit necessarily ingrained in any hunter before they even think about shooting at a wild creature.

But, based on my inspiring experiences with wild creatures after leaving the U.S. Army in 1966, I could never, ever raise a firearm again. The army taught me to shoot to kill, and thank the Lord I never did.

By good fortune, I was not assigned to the Vietnam War, even though my Korean unit, The First Cavalry, was reassigned there while I was in Korea. That occurred months before I was myself transferred to a Washington, D.C., intelligence investigative unit for the remainder of my time in the service.

Why, I ask, should any human being shoot to kill any living being? Some would answer that animals and birds kill humans, so what should protect them from hunters or those acting in self defense?

OK! Maybe Grizzlies and other eaters of humans should be more like vegans! Ha! Remember that those giant bears with the big teeth do eat vegetables as well. "Ants, fruits, moose and plants are a few staples of the Alberta grizzly bear's diet. This new research study was the most comprehensive examination of grizzly bear foods ever conducted in Canada," says Science Daily. (Footnote two)

I become angry when hearing or reading about what I consider ridiculous killings or suggestions to kill wild creatures. Environmental disasters, like wildfires, slaughtering untold numbers of birds, animals, fish and other critters are shocking to the conscience as well.

Often they result from careless, heedless, reckless or criminal human behavior. Of course, many of these wild creature tragedies would never have occurred if more people world-wide had been properly educated to respect nature and all of its wild inhabitants.

The massive oil spills inside Alaska's North Slope by Exxon in 2006 and by BP in the Gulf of Mexico in 2010 were perfect examples of this negligence or total lack of care. The uncounted deaths of wild creatures, birds and fish will impact on those populations possibly forever. Yet the oil companies and politicians are now pressing for a massive oil pipeline, carrying heavy oil from Alberta and Saskatchewan, Canada across the Great Plains to the Gulf of Mexico.

The map of the proposed line reveals the potential adverse impact to soil, water supplies and natural habitats, created by a pipeline leak, could be catastrophic. (Footnote three) Of course, protecting the territories where wild creatures live is one of the lowest priorities for the giant oil companies, many of their customers and most pro-corporate governmental officials.

Here's a typical example of what a low priority some animals' lives have with many politicians and those who vote for them.

"First thing we do, let's kill all the coyotes," headlines a column written by Alex Beam in The Herald Tribune in January 2012. Beam details threats to adults and children from roaming coyotes within, of all places, the City of Boston, Massachusetts, and its suburbs. "

Seven years ago (2005), Michael Striar ran for mayor of Newton, on a kill-the-coyotes platform. He got 42 percent of the vote," writes Beam. However, he continues, when confronted with his old shoot to kill platform, Striar told him that he doesn't advocate such killings, and actually is "very anti-hunting and anti-gun."

Like today, there were traps available to safely remove predator animals to remote areas without harming them.

All killings of wild creatures need to be avoided at all cost, unless a defense against a deadly attack is at stake.

I must confess, however, I am not a vegetarian. As an occasional eater of meat and dairy products, I was shocked watching the film documentary, "Food Inc." by Robert Kenner. (Footnote four) It exposed cruel treatment of big farms' cows and chickens and their mass slaughter of those animals and birds, crammed into fenced off areas and cages. Anyone sensitive to the fates of wild creatures needs to discover local farmers with the kindest of instincts.

The Occupational Safety and Health Administration inspects farms to ensure safety of workers. However, the Food Inc. expose reveals that the U.S. Department of Agriculture, charged with checking on cruelty to farm animals and birds, was not then even close to capable of taking on its full responsibilities.

All farmers and fisheries must be regularly inspected and rated by animal, bird and fish care experts. And, any member of the public aware of cruel farm tactics needs to report them immediately. The news media, as well, needs much more aggressive reporting in depth on not only farm irregularities, but on wide varieties of environmental disasters created by people.

When men, women or children are killed or murdered, public officials and the media sometimes are aggressive in pursuing and exposing the culprits. But, most of the time, little attention focuses on killing of and cruelty to wild creatures.

Only wounded or murdered pets occasionally get such attention when outrage, caused by headline news stories or animal advocacy organizations, demands action against the perpetrator or perpetrators.

Obviously, however, even some of pets' so called care takers need education on the real needs of tamed critters, because their actions become negligent and cruel at times.

One line of attack on consumption of processed foods, meat, fish and dairy products argues, with scientific credibility, that such alleged nourishment can actually cause long term illnesses and deaths from heart attacks, cancer and type two diabetes.

The documentary, "Forks Over Knives," repetitiously and convincingly reveals these fearsome diagnoses. The film, written and directed by Lee Fulkerson, inspires the viewer with eye-riveting evidence that a vegetarian diet can cure those scary diseases and simultaneously assist the dangerously overweight to slim down their horrendously fat bodies. It credits the decades of research work by Dr. T. Colin Campbell, a Cornell University biochemist and Dr. Caldwell Esselstyn, a former top surgeon at the Cleveland Clinic, with these lifesaving discoveries. (Footnote five)

"The Animal Liberation," a book written by Pete Singer, insists humans, as well as all other living creatures, should have equal living rights. Giving humans the rights to live, or live without pain, while excluding wild creatures from those rights is discriminatory, he argues. "It may be objected that comparisons of sufferings of different species are impossible to make, and that for this reason when the interests of animals and human beings clash the principle of equality gives no guidance. It is probably true that comparisons of suffering between members of different species cannot be made precisely, but precision is not essential."

"Even if we were to prevent the infliction of suffering on animals, only when it is quite certain that the interests of human beings will not be affected, we would be forced to make radical changes in our treatment of animals that would involve our diet; the farming methods we use; experimental procedures in many fields of science; our approach to wildlife and to hunting, trapping and the wearing of furs, and areas of entertainment like circuses, rodeos, and zoos. As a result a vast amount of suffering would be avoided."

"Pain and suffering are bad and should he prevented or minimized, irrespective of the race, sex, or species of the being that suffers. How bad a pain is depends on how intense it is and how long it lasts, but pains of the same magnitude are equally bad regardless of species," Singer writes.

In other words: "Animals should be treated in the way that is best for the animals concerned - which may not be the way that suits human beings," says The British Broadcasting Corporation's ethics standards.

Footnote One:

http://www.mannmuseum.com/american-treatment-of-the-indian-tribes/

Footnote Two:

http://www.sciencedaily.com/releases/2007/02/070215083202.htm

Footnote Three:
http://www.transcanada.com/keystone_pipeline_map.html
Footnote Four:
http://www.bing.com/movies/search/synopsis?q=Food%2c+Inc.&id=3724c50e-c564-4222-9cb0-1a658fe30730&FORM=DTPMVO
Footnote Five: www.ForksOverKnives.com

The next two tales are symptomatic of how encounters with animals, birds, and all creatures in the wild can capture humans' hearts forever and convince them kindness is essential.

The Falcon and The Great Blue Heron

Besides being a busy doctor, John Fulkerson is a wine-maker in a countrified setting: old stone walls, rusty red barns, brooks and forests, part of the rolling hills of historical Litchfield, Connecticut. John's grape vines are part of a landscape with a variety of trees and two gentle, rolling fields.

He and his wife, Lynn, an avid gardener, are finely tuned to the sounds and movements of wild animals and birds. John and birds of prey are not strangers. He has watched Hawks, Falcons and Vultures swoop over his neighborhood. These birds, all of varying sizes, have sharp eyes, muscled wings and large talons. They prey on mice, ground squirrels, rabbits, reptiles, and even weak, small birds.

On one particular bright, clear summer day in 2006, John and Lynn were tending to their gardens when John spotted a struggling winged creature adjacent to their netting-enclosed blueberry patch. The desperately struggling bird turned out to be a male Merlin Falcon. It was trapped deep in a tangle of netting protecting the berry patch from heavy bird feasting.

The one-foot tall Falcon, normally so graceful while sliding through the sky or perched on a branch, was anxiously struggling for its life. One of its legs and attached talons had caught on the outside side of the netting. It was hopping around on one leg trying to free the other one. Its small white neck and brown and white-stripped chest showed under the big, hooked beak and large beady eyes. Its two-foot wingspan, light grey-blue on top and stripped brown and white underneath, whacked back and forth under the netting. Its one yellow leg was moving freely despite the netting trap surrounding the bird's other leg.

"I moved with caution toward it because the bird looked angry. Its beak and eyes were wide open. I didn't want to get too close. I thought it might go after me," John says.

So he yelled out for help from Lynn. She hurried into the house. First, she found a book to identify the struggling bird and then a pair of scissors to free it from the netting. John and Lynn initially looked closely at the bird's markings. They identified it as a male Merlin Falcon, formerly known as the pigeon hawk. It is a bird so rarely seen in town that some bird watchers speculated the breed had disappeared entirely from the Litchfield Hills. John surmised the Falcon had spotted prey, like a small bird or frog, below the blueberry netting, dove at it and, instead, entrapped itself.

Having already observed the Falcon's open beak and leg talons moving in its desperate stay-alive struggle, John approached its back or winged side for ultimate safety. Because he is a doctor who specializes in human knees and shoulders, he had some hands on experience with injured limbs before attempting to untangle this falcon. The bird had been fighting for freedom for quite a few minutes while inside this accidental trap.

Naturally, it expressed fear and hostility the closer John approached. It put up a struggle with every part of its being while hopping with its free leg on the other side of the netting. As John began working with the scissors on the netting like a surgeon, the Falcon at first fought his efforts. But soon, the bird began gradually slowing down its struggles. Its beak, ever so gradually, closed, as John looked on. The falcon appeared to tire and relax simultaneously. John felt from the bird's body language that the Falcon had become aware he was working hard to save him, not harm him.

After several minutes, the cautious Doctor John, accustomed to his dormant patients under general anaesthesia, was able to free the initially struggling Falcon. The second John freed the bird, instead of immediately flying away, as John expected, the Falcon sat meekly on the ground. It was so still John was afraid it was dying of dehydration and weakness. "I felt bad. Here was a beautiful bird right in front of me ready to die," he says. "My first instinct then was to run at the bird to scare him off the ground. When I did that, the bird suddenly took off!"

The Falcon, now sporting one talon mangled from its struggles with the wound up netting, flew haltingly into the blue sky above. "But then," John explains, "instead of flying away in fear, it flew up about thirty feet in the air above and circled almost directly above my head before then flying away into a nearby tree line and disappearing."

A summer later, says John, Lynn spotted a falcon, feeding young in a tree. Later, she observed two fledgling Merlin Falcons hopping around awkwardly on two poles supporting the grape vines producing wines. Not long afterward, in separate sightings, they both spotted an adult Merlin Falcon apparently nesting nearby in the back yard.

They were not sure if this bird was the same injured Falcon John had rescued. However, by that time, they learned from a naturalist that a Merlin Falcon can survive and thrive even after mangling the talons on one of its legs. In honor of the Falcons, the Fulkersons' vineyard became "Merlin Meadows."

The Falcon was not John's only brush with a hostile, powerful bird. He and Lynn were eating breakfast overlooking Merlin Meadows one bright, beautiful, clear Saturday 2008 summer morning, when Lynn spotted a Great Blue Heron, fishing in the pond below. "Hey John," she exclaimed, "a Heron's eating breakfast!" It was a beautiful, light blue, prehistoric creature with long legs for fishing that made the winged one between three and four feet high. He had long yellow legs and a narrow head with a matching lengthy dark yellow-brown beak, perfect for spearing underwater targets.

Some 12 years earlier, John stocked the pond with Rainbow Trout. In doing so, he soon attracted regular visits from one Great Blue Heron, or less likely, several other herons anxious to prey on "my" fish.

As time wore on, these visits upset John more and more. He repeatedly rushed down about seventy-five yards to the pond to scare away what he considered one persistent and annoying heron. Herons, like this one, walk haltingly and patiently on their long, stick-like legs. The birds proceed ever so slowly while stopping to scan the waters for fish. Listening, they gaze straight ahead. Occasionally, herons crane their necks to look up in the air and check out sounds above. They are somewhat accustomed to humans frightening them away from their prey, as John was repeatedly doing.

John decided he needed a wanted poster of the Great Blue Heron. Just kidding! (Photo By John Fulkerson)

One day, John spotted the heron hunting once again along the pond. Suddenly and startlingly, John watched as it caught its breakfast, a struggling trout it held, with seeming pride, inside its beak. John was livid! He raced down the hill toward the spot where the Heron had been wading. As he approached, the impervious heron walked out of the water to the shore. The big-winged creature was now ready to eat his meal, or perhaps save it in his beak for a more private breakfast or lunch. The live, wounded fish vibrated in his beak.

 John, now nearby, yelled and waved a stick at the heron, scaring it into the air. Like a slow motion plane taking off with too much to carry in the way of luggage, the heron strained its engines, flapping, flapping and flapping. It finally rose several feet into the air and veered away from John as he chased after it.

The heron flew low through a gap in the trees across one small field, and into the far end of another. There it momentarily perched in one of the trees adjacent to the field. The trees around and above the Heron were high enough to prevent a fast exit, particularly with the weight of the trout in its beak.

Meanwhile, John had picked up a couple of one-inch diameter stones in anticipation of scaring it. Before he could follow the bird into the second field, it flew out of its perch and headed right back across that second field toward John, who couldn't believe the bird's moxie. As the heron began to fly right by John in the tree gap between the two fields, John threw one of the stones in a line he estimated was too far in front to hit it. As it turned out, the stone passed about 10 yards in front of the Heron's head, causing it "to drop the trout practically at my feet!" says John. "That was a conquest!" John explains, "This was my territory not his."

The heron then rose gradually, but as rapidly as it could into the open sky! It finally disappeared. Meanwhile, John ran to the spot where the fish dropped, grabbed its slimy body and carried it up hill to the house. The deliciously cooked trout became an unexpected breakfast treat for his wife Lynn and himself, instead of a raw one for the obviously disappointed Heron.

In the summer of 2009, John was peering down at the trout pond when he spotted either the same Great Blue Heron or another one standing at one end of the pond eating a fish. As he had dozens of times over the years, John ran down toward the waterside screaming and waving a walking stick, but this time the bird didn't fly away immediately. When John was about 20 feet away, he still could see the heron standing his ground, and looking curiously at him. "I actually felt concerned about his boldness," he says.

So he picked up a small stick from the ground and threw it in the general direction of the bird. The heron vibrated up and flew away slowly, but looked right at him. Within seconds, the heron veered around and flew right at John, flying about 50 feet over his head. "It really scared me," he exclaimed.

As a result of his experiences, John believes that birds interact with people in ways that startle the imagination. Their body language, their mannerisms and sounds communicate appropriately, either a necessary friendly or hostile message toward humans, coming into close contact with them.

They may not have the words humans have, but they have their own basic means to tell humans what they feel about them, or to elucidate the circumstances confronting them. "I believe there is a level of communication with creatures that we understand poorly," says John. "Those of us fortunate enough to be close to wild creatures in a harmonious relationship (even a little friendly competition is harmonious) are fortunate to experience relationship and communication with wild creatures. They are not so different from us, and they are smarter in some ways. They do not pretend to know what they do not understand!"

What is truly fascinating and tale-delicious arrives when big birds decide to build a nest smack in the middle of a busy city spot where scores of people see them live their lives, comprising the bringing up their young feathery ones.

The next tale follows the travails of a family of Red-tailed Hawks as they build a large, round stick nest right on top of an eagle sculpture on the corner of a city courthouse.

Hawks Nesting In The City Find Tragedy and Inspire Humans as Fans

Most people, walking in any city, pay so little attention to wild, beautiful birds, unless the winged creatures decide to become theatrical.

One of the most famed examples is the Red-tailed Hawk, known as Pale Male. He and his female companion were initially and intentionally frightened away from a New York City Central Park nest, only to opt instead for a roost high up on the ledge of a Fifth Avenue apartment house. It became a controversial perch among apartment dwellers living underneath.

Representatives of the apartment's co-op initially dismantled the nest. However, an immediate and huge international public protest forced apartment owners to reset the nest back on the ledge.

This story's various episodes have dragged on excitingly for years. A permanent telescope was situated in the park so anyone who wanted could spy on the hawks' activity. Scintillating photos of Pale Male and spouses, as well as a year-to-year diary, are readily available on a fascinating Internet site. (Footnote one)

Another less publicized single episode-adventure entailed the mother Mallard whose ducklings were whirled into a Newcastle, England, sewer line. Undaunted, mother feather flashed, waddled and tracked after their sounds. She barrelled along the streets above the sewer pipe until she reached a dead end that turned out to be a manhole. Mom quacked with alarm. She hung out nervously for hours on top of the manhole cover, until neighbors finally became attracted to her. They then detected sounds of her six young ones below, before rescuing them, according to a dramatic news story in The Daily Mail. (Footnote two)

Aside from reading awe-inspiring news stories about these bird adventures, there is nothing like being constantly in the midst of one with several daily or weekly chapters. It moves most humans outside of myriads of other thoughts, as well as their egos, into the purer, wilder, more exciting world of nature.

I experienced an awesome feathered tale only once in my long career as a newsman. Since then the story, unlike thousands of other news sagas, has never left me. I first wrote about it in July 2000. Afterward, I verbally spun it to friends endlessly. So now you will get it too!

I was the reporter regularly assigned to cover the two Hartford Superior Courts within view of the State Capitol Building, its lush park and the State Supreme Court/State Library edifice in Connecticut's Capitol City of Hartford. I either drove or walked to courts daily during the working week from the newspaper's office two blocks away. The most fascinating of scoops, including headlined prosecutions of rioters, murderers and corrupt politicians, evolved through the adventures of family of wild, normally countrified, hawks.

I recall the first time they came to my attention. I had just arrived outside court, ready to cover all sorts of news inside.

Outside, Courant photographer, now freelancer Bob MacDonnell, had set up his telephoto camera on a tripod, and was focusing for what seemed like minutes on what I thought was the roof of the old courthouse. (Footnote three)

I must have made a wisecrack about how fascinating the roof's shingles must be. However, he calmly glanced at me incredulously for a second or two, and then, saying not a word, turned to point his index finger up toward the building's eves.

Immediately my eyes riveted on mother and father red-tailed hawks hanging around their large stick-filled nest. More enticing yet, the nest was constructed by those hawks on top of a three-foot eagle sculpture, embedded into the upper corner of that old, attractive Superior Court House.

The hawks had constructed their craggy nest-ball just feet behind the stern looking concrete eagle's head and its wings. It was largely centered behind the eagle's right wing. Right-wingers would not have approved. White bird dung was already streaking down the head, neck, wings and body of the eagle. A live eagle, had it observed the activity would never have put up with such a hawk nest placement on its statute! As well, some frequenters of the court with traditionalist tastes didn't approve of the hawks' concept of home.

Later, I heard, building purists and protectors, including perhaps a judge or two, complained that the hawks could be damaging the significant historic building's beautiful sculpture. But, bird lovers inside and outside of civil court, and the directly adjacent criminal court, had too powerful a public lobby for anyone to challenge, even the opposing historians, art lovers or judges. Indeed, all of those bird fans had cause to be proud the building was holding and protecting this cozy nest.

The court, itself, now handling civil cases only, is an historical treasure to those admiring it from all angles, outside and inside.

"It blended beau-arts classicism and art deco styles into the imposing structure. It was designed by the architectural firms of Paul P. Cret of Philadelphia and Smith & Bassette of Hartford," according to research gathered by State Librarian Stephen Rice. "The four-story, rectangular new Courthouse (completed in 1929 and costing over $28 million) contained 15 different kinds of marbles in its interior. They ranged from the soft St. Memy stone from the coast of Normandy, France to pink Tennessee marble," says Rice.

Inside the main chamber, leading to three ground floor courtrooms, is a ceiling, close to cathedral in style, and a generous corridor inviting lawyers and their clients to hang around an inside snack stand, negotiate their cases, or just talk about any gossip they please. News reporters too enjoy capturing news sources there and interviewing them in the open, despite an occasional and distracting echo or two.

Outside, in front of the south courthouse wall, MacDonnell told me he was spending as much time as he could each day photographing the hawks as they flew in and out of the nest and up into the sky above.

Of course, his descriptions of the hawk action immediately convinced me that I too would commit to compliment his photos with a feature story I knew I was going to love writing. Although I had been a Courant reporter for decades, I had never even dreamed I would write such a fascinating nature article. Feature stories weren't my specialty; rather, hard news and investigatory articles on government and corporate corruption were more down my alley.

Here is the story compiled by MacDonnell and myself for The Hartford Courant through several weeks of observations! Some additional details, not included in the original article, I compiled from memory. MacDonnell's photos, taken over many hours of waiting for just the right shot, were dramatically telling, enhancing the article beyond all words.

The baby hawks watched by one of their parents, as they explore their Eagle nesting area. (Courant Photo by Bob MacDonnell) (Footnote four)

In fact, MacDonnell covered every phase of the extraordinary story with critical lens shots.

For months, the struggles of a family of red-tailed hawks nesting atop Hartford Superior Court have rivaled any courtroom drama unfolding inside.

The spectacle — the birth of two chicks over Easter weekend, the death of their mother a week later and the father hawk raising the fledglings alone — has captured the attention of court clerks, jurors, uniformed sheriffs, lawyers in business suits, passers by and neighborhood residents all spring.

Daily, dozens of people gathered along Washington Street, craning their necks for views of the hawks, nesting on an eagle sculpture at the civil court. Some camera buffs take photo after photo. Spectators stand and stare with a few training binoculars on the birds' activities. Then, most immediately gapers begin fast and furious detailed conversations about the hawks with anyone they can find nearby.

Late last month (June 2000), the fledglings, after hopping around a bit next to the nest, began flying in and out of it, sometimes disappearing for minutes and hours at a time.

The nest is vacant now. A sheriff recently saw one of the youngsters fall off a park tree branch next to the court, hit the ground and flap around until airborne again. Some regular onlookers are feeling like sad empty nesters. "My God, I feel like my kid is going off to college," said Brenda Pierscinski, a court clerk.

On the third floor in the adjacent Lafayette Street criminal court, court stenographers set up a small telescope for employees to watch the hawk soap opera. Once outsiders and insiders heard about it, others flocked to train their eyes for long minutes into the scope.

One close observer and court insider said she is looking for a photo of one of the hawks so she can create "hawking justice" T-shirts for the "legal eagles" in the courthouse.

"In a crazy sort of way, it brings people together," Elaine Halloran, a veteran criminal court clerk, said. "People keep asking one another: 'What are (the hawks) doing today?' "

The broad, rounded, brown winged birds with short, wide red tails began building the bulky nest in February. Their courtship rituals, including flight demonstrations and piercing screams, quickly drew much attention. By late March, the female had laid eggs and was incubating them, along with the male. They hunted in the court's adjacent small park and beyond, periodically returning to the nest with food for their two youngsters. These hawks can capture "rodents, rabbits, birds, reptiles, and sometimes fish or large insects," says BirdWeb.

Soon after the chicks hatched, their airborne mother, while being harassed by noisy crows, was severely injured when she struck what some believed was the nearby mammoth Connecticut Supreme Court building or a nearby tree. Barbara Chappell, a court administrative assistant, found the injured bird on the ground near the Supreme Court. She called a "wildlife rehabilitator" to care for it, but after being carefully picked up and cared for, the hawk died the next day.

Now, the male hawk was sadly alone without his mate, the mother, to care for the chicks — tiny white balls of down barely a week old. More Crows, natural enemies of raptors, harassed him, sometimes making it difficult for him to stray from the nest to hunt. Sounds from raspy, swarming cars and trucks, puffing exhaust fumes, in the morning and evening city traffic rush didn't help him.

Regular hawk-watchers became alarmed, especially after construction workers, using a huge ear-popping crane, began repairing and tarring the roof directly above the nest. Court personnel, distressed about the construction disruption and seeking advice, placed at least a half dozen calls to the state Department of Environmental Protection, the Audubon Society and other organizations.

Worried the hawk chicks would not survive without their mother amid all the nearby street traffic, building construction and potential other city dangers, some observers asked state environmental officials whether they could provide food for the hawks, or remove the chicks from the nest and raise them in captivity.

But, those suggestions were soundly rejected. "We thought Dad would do fine, and it was best not to intervene, and that proved wise," said Chris Vann, a biologist for the DEEP Wildlife Division. Experts confirm that both male and female Red-tailed Hawks care for their chicks, while the male collects prey to feed his mate and the chicks.

Nevertheless, inside and outside both courthouses employees and spectators alike regularly argued over whether a male hawk had the ability and staying power to care for his young. Many of the females in the daily nature audience for those bird adventures had their doubts and relayed constant worries about the chicks to anyone who would listen. Those concerned women were constantly harangued by he-males. They insisted Daddy birds are just as capable as Daddy humans to care for their young as Moms are.

As the drama developed for concerned observers, the male hawk, during the heart of the day, could be viewed regularly perched on the top southeast corner of an abandoned, nearby 14- story office building. He was seeking out prey in the small courtside park below, while also glancing laterally downward at the nesting chicks, almost a football field's length in the distance.

"There are a lot of human fathers who could learn a lot from him," Halloran said. "He's quite a hawk. When the crows came to dive at him, he just stayed there, regally, without a move."

In mid-June, the larger of the two fledglings, a female, hopped off the nest to an adjacent ledge. Late in the afternoon, a gust of wind caught the young bird, knocking it from the ledge. It floated 30 or 40 feet and landed on a judge's black Suburban auto. It hooked a claw in the car's back door hinge, but someone walking by quickly freed it, and it continued hopping along the car's roof.

Soon a heated dispute broke out among several court employees before and after two of them used an article of clothing to move the bird to a tree next to traffic laden Washington Street. The argument ensued among the civil court clerks, working for the judge whose car the hawk landed upon, and the criminal court clerks from the neighboring court, who had become very protective of the hawk family.

The judge's clerks demanded the hawk be taken off their boss' car, while their antagonists insisted the bird be left to its own desires and instincts.

Court clerk Holly Scalzo, who had been closely monitoring the hawks for weeks, yelled at the two judge's clerks to leave the bird alone. "I can't take this any more! It's getting to be too much," she exclaimed painfully.

As the battle developed further, the judge's clerks went inside the courthouse to retrieve a coat they used to corral the hawk and carry it to a small tree branch of a tree, directly adjacent to busy Washington Street. They were immediately and heavily criticized by the criminal court clerks, who insisted the baby bird might fly down to the street or across it, and get hit by a car during hectic late afternoon traffic. One of the hawk lovers once again called state environmentalists to complain.

Vann, the state wildlife man, already sucked into the controversy earlier, was urged to return to the scene. Clerks waited for him for quite a while after the court closed. Then, mistaking his approach to the hawk's tree perch as one of an interloper, they yelled for him to stay away. But, Vann quickly soothed the concerned clerks with his identity.

He initially chased the bird a short distance along the street before capturing it. Then, he received official courthouse permission to mount himself to the roof with the hawk to return it to the nest. He said the bird was uninjured, but predicted it might happen again. The birds did from time to time jump from the nest to the roof, but were always able to return to the nest.

"It's touch and go! A lot of young birds get themselves into trouble. This is a difficult time for them," Vann said.

Red-tailed hawks are the most common and adaptable raptors in Connecticut. Although they usually nest in wooded areas near open fields, they will adapt to various nesting habitats, even in urban settings, to try to catch their quarry with emphasis on rats, mice, squirrels and pigeons.

Hartford residents Richard Hernandez and Marsha Banas have appreciated the sight of the hawks in the city. They used to check on the chicks with their binoculars while walking along Washington Street.

``We live in the neighborhood and came by every day to check their progress,'' Hernandez said. ``It's something you don't normally see in the city. It's great for Hartford. ''

This was not a story so much about birds communicating with people, although such interaction was not unlikely. Rather, it was a tale of some extremely concerned people attempting to read the minds of a family of hawks whose trials and troubles involved a life and death struggle to survive.

Footnote one:
http://www.palemale.com/feb2305.html

Footnote two:
http://www.dailymail.co.uk/news/article-1026801/Amazing-rescue-mother-duck-went-extra-mile.html

Footnote three: http://www.macdonnellphoto.com/

Footnote four: Hartford Courant Sunday, July 09, 2000 HANGIN' WITH THE HAWKS A HARTFORD SAGA OF LIFE AND DEATH, Story Copyrighted by The Hartford Courant

Living through and writing that cliffhanger, or rather ledge-hanger, as a reporter was so much fun! I guess I was so happy because I never expected my bird feeding and nature loving days as a little kid to become part of my story telling life as a news reporter.

The next tale shows how enchanting birds can be to one who listens to them and heeds their commands.

Hummingbird Tea

For most of nearly seven decades of life, I have fed the birds with a variety of feeders, while fighting off constant intrusions by acrobatic Grey Squirrels. As I wrote earlier, they jump over man-made barriers, flip onto the vibrating feeders and then eat like pigs! Fortunately, plastic-tubed hummingbird feeders are not one of their targets.

Hummingbirds, when hungry, have their own brand of quiet aggression. They have even been known to suck honey water out of a tube held by a patient bird lover's hand.

More recently, Bob and Dorothy Knox, our friends and married former next-door neighbors, gave my wife, Ina, a gardener fond of flowers, a hummingbird feeder for her birthday. I cannot ever remember having one. My feeders were all of the birdseed variety, not the ones holding sweet water for hummingbirds.

Since I was a young boy, I've always been fascinated by their exotic looks and incredible speed. So Ina and I began having regular fun observing their feeding habits while gazing out of the window or while relaxing on the porch. We tried to make sure their feeder was filled with appetizing sugar water. They are the jets of flying creatures. They don't run out of gas either, like airline jets and helicopters do. Can you imagine that when winter starts to threaten, these diminutive birds fly from Canada and New England to Mexico, Northern Panama or Nicaragua? Check it out! (Footnote one)

The males' ruby throats are offset with greenish-grey caps, white breasts, a greenish grey under body, a shiny green back and greyish wings. Females are less spectacular with a light green back and whitish-grey throat.

Once on the wing, never do they stay long in one place unless they are feeding in clumps of flowers or at a feeder. When finished sucking in the sweets, their wings, so fast moving they are blurs, propel them out and away within a second or two. They perform 60 to 80 wing beats in a second and have 1,220 heartbeats per minute while flying, says Operation Rubythroat. (Footnote two)

If a human or animal approaches, they can, and often do, become vaporous through incredible speed. They can fly upside down or backwards. Each day they suck in twice their two to six gram body weights daily to absorb enough energy to fly.

As I sat upstairs at home, gazing at my computer screen on a bright sunny day, I was compelled to change focus by mysterious flashy movements. I look up from an Internet search into the window right in front of me on the second floor of our antique, saltbox home. Only four or five feet away, just about five feet below the gable of the shingled roof, was a female ruby throated hummingbird hovering, hovering, and hovering.

She refused to fly away. Every so often the little one darted upward and within seconds dropped downward, its green wings moving so fast they were almost invisible. The tiniest bird in North America was seemingly staring right at me. Up and down, back and forth this female moved. Her eyes continually appeared to meet mine. I became momentarily hypnotized

This was a show far more enticing than the nature musicals on Broadway or Disney World! The beautiful flying creature's throat was all white with brownish tint, unlike its beautiful ruby throated male partner. The bird was bobbing and weaving there, seemingly for a minute, although it probably was 30 to 45 seconds. But, in hummingbird time, it was indeed bird-minutes before it finally and abruptly zipped upward, backward and sideways to disappear.

At least in my experience, seldom do hummingbirds stay and gaze through a window that long with a human close by, gaping right back at it on the opposite side. Hundreds of times since my childhood days, I have watched with utter fascination through windows and outside in the open air, as hummingbirds jet within milliseconds from place to place.

But, while feeding inside a flower or a hummingbird feeder, the little creatures do make exceptions to stay a while. And, oh, yes, if you become an affection-ado and watch very carefully, once in a while you spot them perching on a tree limb, sometimes for quite a while in hummingbird time. Always, when they leave from any spot, they disappear so swiftly, they seem like a mirage, dream, or a beautiful mind figment.

As I – mesmerized - watched this female, I could not help having the unmistakable feeling the little one was communicating with me. As I thought more about that, there was only one message making sense.

Below the window, out of sight to the right of a roof gable are the home's porch and a little white flowering tree nearby. There on one of its lowest branches hangs the hummingbird feeder. It's a little curved clear plastic bottle with a wider red round bottom and four fake yellow flowers around its base complete with tiny holes in their midst, allowing birds to suck in the sugar water created for them.

Immediately after my face-to-face with the fluttering beauty, I rushed downstairs and sure enough the feeder was empty. Instantaneously, I brought it inside, boiled water with sugar in a pot, filled up the plastic bottle with that hummingbird juice, and returned to hang it up in its usual spot. It sure wouldn't be long, I thought, before the Hummingbird visits started up again. And, the first visitor, I recall, was a female. Although I could not be sure, it had to be the one who made sure I knew the feeder was empty.

Days later, Ina, my wife, invited our friends, Jan and Maletta, a Swedish couple, and another close friend, Norrie, whose wife, Trudie, was then overseas in Scotland, to tea on the porch. It was a lovely drink-feast: two teapots with green tea and black tea, a plumb tart and some blueberry muffin-cake. The sun was shinning brightly on a day just short of fall with a slightly chilly breeze.

The porch looked out on a small lawn. Some distant flowerbeds are in the background near a small brook, then beyond on the stream's far side, a small former cattle-feeding field, bounded alternately by a stonewall and a barbed wire fence. Close at hand to the tea party was the white flowering tree, a Rose of Sharon, holding the hummingbird feeder, and two nearby hanging flowerpots, including pink Petunias and white and purple annuals, dangling from a porch hook. As we all talked, two hummingbirds flew over us, parallel levels by us and around us and into the feeder nearby. Sometimes they zipped seemingly less than a foot over our heads. Often they alternated their teatime treats from the feeder to flying darts into the potted flowers hanging on the porch near us.

Our constant talk seemingly never bothered them; nor did it startle the other birds or the wild animals respectively moving through, the air, the woods and field nearby. One hundred yards below us, a magnificent Great Blue Heron flew off the brook and dodged a host of tree limbs as its large wingspan pumped and swerved it upward.

That slow, deliberate flight came not long before a reddish brown coyote walked along the opposite side of that same brook not far away from the spot where the long-legged heron had been fishing. However, the coyote, soon trotting away, eventually disappearing into nearby woods, apparently did not scare off two female deer, one a teenager and the other, possibly her mother, who soon ambled by the brook-side while eating field grass.

As long as I have lived, I have never, ever seen this many animals and birds come into view one after the other in our backyard! Long after the deer had sauntered on, the hummingbirds continued feeding near us and disappearing to reappear to feed again either into the feeder's fake yellow flowers or the real ones hanging nearby. Frequently, they darted up in the air well over our heads. But, when they played with one another, that is when they zipped over us, just feet away from our startled eyes. They disappeared and reappeared within seconds.

What a contrast, I thought: jet stream hummingbird flights and the slow dinosaur-like aerial take off of the Great Blue Heron! Both have their own beauty! Indelible in my mind are the 15 to 20 minute airborne antics of all those hummingbirds. Again! They were often just inches or feet above the tea party participants' heads, as all of us chatted and laughed. Our noise level would normally encourage the average wild bird or animal to dart off into the woods or fields nearby. But that day, mysteriously, it did not.

My tale of the hummingbirds' interplay with my family and friends is tame compared with one photographed and recounted on YouTube.

In June 2007, a Saratoga, Californian couple, Peter Tommerup and Lee Anne Welch, rescued a baby hummingbird. The little hummingbird girl damaged a wing falling out of its nest. The couple nursed it before sending it on to the Sulfur Creek Nature Center in Hayward, California. After two weeks of care, the center released the little bird safely into the wild.

At one point, Mr. Tommerup put the baby hummingbird in his cupped hand to await its mother's potential interaction. Mom soon arrived in a twitter. She, after zooming overheard several times, swooped down and ultimately fed the little one still in Mr. Tommerup's hand! It is all on video, photographed by Gary Breitbard. (Footnote three)

A friend and former editor of mine, Jim Smith, after hearing about my interest in interconnections among wild birds and people, referred me to his daughter, Barbara Ann Davis. She tells this fascinating story of interplay among her two young sons, herself and a trapped hummingbird.

Here is her story:

"The boys and I were returning home. I had just pulled the minivan into the garage. We were getting out of the car when I immediately noticed a hummingbird flying along the garage's white ceiling. It was bumping it every so often in its attempts to find a way out. Two of the large garage doors were open. It was very sunny outside, so I thought it would figure out how to escape, but it didn't."

"I got the video camera, and the boys decided that the bird wanted to live with us so they ran to find 'nest' materials. I videotaped the bird for a while. Then, it landed on one of the garage door opener things attached to the ceiling."

"The boys had come back. We decided to try to help it find its way outside. The first thing I tried was a hockey stick. I reached up with it and didn't try to touch the fragile little thing, but put it next to him. It wasn't interested."

"Then I got the stepladder and placed it underneath the ceiling. I climbed up fully expecting the bird to take off again, but it didn't. It just sat there (on a ceiling perch), looking right at me. I am sure it was exhausted, but it seemed alert and aware of my being so close. I slowly reached up my hands and put one underneath, touching its foot. It released the metal support it was clinging to and climbed onto my hand. I put my other hand over it and climbed back down, totally surprised at how easy it was."

"The boys were uncharacteristically calm, and we walked outside. I told the boys that when I moved my hand, the little thing would zip away. They peeked into my cupped hands first, and then I slowly moved my hand. The bird just sat there."

"Each boy very gently stroked its head with a finger. We remarked on its long beak, and I was explaining how fast their hearts beat. Finally, after abut a minute, it took off and zipped up to a tree. It was flying a bit slower than usual I think, but still seemed to be healthy and maybe even happy to be back in a tree."

Footnote one:

http://www.hiltonpond.org/ArticleHummerMigrationMain.html

Footnote two:
http://www.rubythroat.org/RTHUFactsMain.html/

Footnote three:
http://livesteaua.com/view/l7xBLvMIBZU/peter-peeps-rescued-baby-hummingbird-fed-in-hand-by-mother/

Speaking of birds, here is a tale of one of the largest, most beautiful flying creatures in the universe. Take a look at this mountainous flight below! It's twenty of the beauties flying over snow-capped mountains. Here is the amazing photo, by Ben Hall Photography, as seen on the Internet. (Footnote one alpha).

The Adventures and Wild Flights of Eilish

It was another spectacular color action photo of a magnificent bird on the front page of The Hartford Courant. A fast moving video immediately popped up inside my imagination. The beautiful pink, 20-year-old, Chilean Flamingo with black wing epaulets was going airborne. It skimmed along the surface of the Connecticut River near an East Haddam State Park.

Here is the dramatic and beautiful photo of that Chilean Flamingo, known as either Eilish or Elisha, flying in Haddam State Park on the Connecticut River. (Hartford Courant and ctphotojournalist.com photo)

The closer I looked, the more the fascination. From curved head to toes, the beauty looked about four feet high. Its five-foot wingspan was in full flap. Its webbed feet simultaneously ran and grazed the water's surface, an amazing take off operation. Bushes, tall grass and trees on the river's waterline were a blur. This beautiful, wild flight was shown in The Hartford Courant photo, above, published October 1, 1997. (Footnote one)

Unfortunately, this female's energy was in the wrong place at the right time. The Connecticut River Valley is part of the Atlantic Flyway, one of four large migratory bird flyways in North America. However, in the fall, most bird species there are flying south to escape the winter, while this Flamingo ultimately flew to the freezing north in Ontario, Canada.

Her Chilean south to north migration habits probably influenced her flying directions. However, if she flew south, instead of north, and disappeared into her home grounds with her old friends, the world would never have enjoyed her newsy adventures.

Possibly, airborne flocks of Canadian Geese, whose honking noises are vaguely similar to her own, might have lured her gradually northward. But, geese don't have the Flamingo's long legs and thin blood vessels, features compelling Flamingos to stand on one leg to keep it warmer and conserve body heat. (Footnote two) Geese can handle cold weather, but Flamingos are too slim and tender to handle it.

The Flamingo's story soon became a bewitching nature mystery, The Hartford Courant's news story insisted. None of those on shore or off who observed the impressively sized bird, or heard about its travels knew where it originated. Certainly, late September winds in 1997 were not strong enough to blow the prehistoric-looking creature to Connecticut from its breed's haunts in South American climes.

Its forbearers began existence millions of years ago. Flamingos' ungainly appearances certainly match scientific theory: dinosaurs grew wings and evolved into ungainly flying creatures.

No area zoos or parks or sanctuaries had by then, the first of October 1997, reported a missing Flamingo.

I was sure it must have escaped from my deceased Uncle Dillon Ripley's bird sanctuary and duck ponds, founded for nature conservation and preserving endangered species. They are just a half minute's sparrow's flight from my home down tree-lined Duck Pond Road in Litchfield.

"Wow," I thought, "that Flamingo take off spot is more than 45 minutes by fast car from that Livingston-Ripley Sanctuary here."

I wondered: "How did it fly away?"

Its wings had to be partly clipped to deter flight like the other ducks, geese and another Flamingo inside the fenced in sanctuary. Later, I learned that it escaped with a few powerful flaps just before her wings were to be re-clipped after she moulted.

My instinctive hunch about the bird's captive home derived, along with simple logic, from teenaged experience during the floods of 1955. They were called by a state flood committee report "the worst flood in the history of the eastern United States."

My Uncle Dillon's duck ponds, created when he was but a boy, became overwhelmed by the once in a millennium meeting of two parallel flooded brooks. They are eighth of a mile apart, but with flooding, merged together into the midst of the ponds. Many of the sanctuary's wing clipped ducks and geese escaped by merely paddling with the water flow down stream. Flamingos were not sanctuary inhabitants back then.

My mission then, along with others, later recorded in a book Uncle Dillon wrote, was to patch up fence netting, and later wade into all sorts of swollen brook waters to attempt captures of all the ducks that had not floated far away, in the direction of the massive nearby Ripley Swamp to the south.

Uncle Dillon, I, and others were armed with netted poles. It was a tad dangerous. High rubber boot walking in flooded streams with varying depths, occasionally and without warning, can drop your entire body under rushing waters into short, but deep chasms. That was worrisome a couple of times, because I did not know how fast I was floating after falling, and I knew I could hit rocks on the bottom, or hidden tree limbs flooded under the stream's surface.

At one point, I became overwhelmed with sadness. My pet Springer Spaniel, Topper, a good swimmer with webbed feet, drowned right in front of me. Without warning, he jumped into the stream and disappeared from sight under a collapsed bridge a hundred yards from my home.

Much later, after my dog's deadly tragedy and my futile, tear-filled search for him had faded, I could not resist bragging to my friends that my Uncle Dillon mentioned me in his book, A Paddling of Ducks. "That first frantic work of patching (holes in the fence), done so unstintingly by Dottie (Ripley, Dillon's sister-in-law) and Dennis (Williams), undoubtedly saved many inhabitants of the pond," Dillon wrote.

Naturally, then, I immediately became emotional on first viewing that page-one escaped Flamingo news photo in The Courant. It flashed vivid memories of my and others' past bird rescuing adventures at Dillon's duck pond.

Almost immediately after dropping the newspaper in shock, I telephoned an editor at The Courant. I exclaimed that the Flamingo had to have originated from my uncle's duck pond. A reporter, he told me, had, that very day, learned that the Flamingo's home was indeed was at Dillon's pond, now called the Livingston-Ripley Sanctuary.

Tomorrow a follow up story was ready for the headlines, he said. Well, as it turned out, the first few Courant articles were merely the beginning of a mass of stories, which eventually spread worldwide, on the Internet. China! Egypt! Great Britain! With a little inquiry, the press discovered the bird's keepers baptized her as Eilish, although some called her Eilisha.

Within days, Eilish had roamed far north to Ontario, Canada. There she created unimaginable attention from the populace below her flights or those curious onlookers watching from the shores of lakes and streams as she walked, dipped and ate.

Flamingos usually travel long distances on cloudless nights with tail winds. They can fly as far as 370 miles a trip, at over 35 mph. (Footnote three) This Flamingo's travels, sadly, had to be lonely and sometimes frighteningly frigid. Dangerous too! Chilean Flamingos normally hang out in muddy waters and fly together by the dozens. It nurtures their social skills, saves flying energy and better protects them from flying predators like hawks or eagles.

If a dozen or more of their long pink bodies with curved heads, sporting little curved black beaks, are flying the daytime, the sight is breathtaking. When their black and pink wings flap in formation up in a clear blue sky, it becomes indelibly engraved in a nature lover's long-term memory.

Chilean Flamingos form colonies in temperate zones from central Peru through the Andes and Uruguay to Tierra del Fuego Uruguay, Bolivia, Peru, Argentina and Chile.

So Canada, of course, proved colder than this wandering Flamingo ever imagined. Flamingos love to frequent shallow, muddy water along seacoasts, ponds and sometimes into wetlands near steep mountain ranges. Three front webbed toes help her and her friends navigate and stir up fields of mud along water's edge. Canada offered some similar friendly environs, but Eilish would have to be satisfied squeaking and honking at Canadian Geese and other cold air water birds, who unlike her, enjoyed frigid air and water.

Nevertheless, there's plenty of cold mud, as well as food in the form of crustaceans, frogs, small fish, seeds, and algae around the Ontario ponds, streams and ponds where this Flamingo ultimately flew. Certainly, Eilish's white and black large curved bill would be ready for all the nourishment it could uncover.

During such a long flight, close to 460 miles, she must have hungrily imagined gulping small fishes down into her long neck and from thence into her ample belly.

As Eilish flew, observers below had to be startled and amazed when they saw this large, thin pink and white, pink and black winged Flamingo's long body swoop by. Her wing plumage on the backside edge is black turning to crimson, then becoming pinkish white towards the front edge. The two long legs, tucked underneath as she flew, are green-grey to light blue with dark pink joints, and at the very leg-end, bright pink webbed feet.

Her people-observed moves soon began to be closely reported by Ontario other news media. Eventually, the mystery of her visit and travels moved onto the international Internet news cycles, where millions of children and adults followed her adventures daily.

The paper with the hottest fascination and most detailed coverage for the story was The Ottawa Citizen, naturally since Eilish became a regular paddler and diner inside the Ottawa River.

Soon after her arrival, the paper began reporting the daily attempts by a well-known and dedicated bird rescuer, Kathy Nihei, to capture Eilish and save her from the eventual, perhaps even deadly, dangers of frigid weather approaching.

By now, Eilish had been on a lark for a month and a half. That is an amazingly wild existence for a bird raised for years in a bird sanctuary, well protected and fed inside a warm enclosure in winter. Naturally then, Ms. Nihei, known as "The Bird Woman," was all the more anxious to rescue her from the elements.

Kathy Nihei admiring one of her many patients. (Photo taken by Tony Beck from http://harmonyhopes.blogspot.com/search?q=Kathy+Nihei+*)*

Her love for and care for birds, starting with months of care for a hummingbird, run into by a car in 1981, is legendary in Ontario. Sixteen years later, Eilish could not have wished for more loving persons than Ms. Nihei and her bird center members to save her life.

Eventually, for 25 years, Ms. Nihei's devotion, as well as the bird club members' dedication, had rescued thousands of birds from near death. Ms. Nihei, like many others, believed in the spiritual communications among humans and birds.

"Her eyes still looking into mine, two souls touching," Ms. Nihei wrote as she unsuccessfully tried to nurse an eagle back to health on Christmas Day 1994. "It haunts me still," she said of her hours of close up first aid for the majestic bird, trapped in a wolf snare for two days before being rescued by the snare's tender.

Ms. Nihei, 65, herself, died in January 2009. (Footnote four)

Here is a picturesque description of her wild creature saviour facility, The Wild Bird Center, from freelance writer Moira Farr writing for Onnature:

"On this humid spring day, as I am led by Nihei through the sprawling one-story centre, down a series of narrow hallways and into bright room after room, each filled with cages, perches and tubs catering to different sized birds at different stages of healing, (and the windowless isolation room for birds that might carry communicable diseases), I am serenaded by the urgent "feed me" squawks of baby starlings, robins and grackles, trilling of songbirds and soft coos of mourning doves. Two screech owlets stare with huge eyes from their cage."

"A kestrel with 'feather damage' sits and watches from a pile of egg cartons on top of a fridge, in a room where staff and volunteers prepare food for the avian residents. An albino robin – a permanent resident that was pushed from its nest by rejecting parents – flutters around an enclosure with a killdeer and several grosbeaks. In the insectivore ward, smaller songbirds – a cardinal, a baby bluebird and a bohemian waxwing – bounce around while injuries heal."

So Elisha was simply one of the scores of amazing rescues accomplished by Ms. Nihei!

Headlines Ottawa Citizen Saturday November 22, 1997: "Close, But No Flamingo – Rescuers get within two metres of Elisha" (Her Canadian handle).

Reporter Dave Mullington wrote: "Kathy Nihei added three new tools to her arsenal in the hunt for Elisha the elusive Flamingo yesterday. But Elisha remains free. The director of the Wild Bird Care Centre in Nepean used taped Flamingo bird calls, a remote-controlled Canada goose decoy and a 10 metre-wide spring-loaded net in an attempt to catch the bird at Andrew Haydon Park on the Ottawa River in Nepean. But, just as her rescuers closed in, Elisha decided to take a stroll." (Footnote five)

The bird center had been trying to trap Eilish since she was first sighted at that same nature park more than two weeks earlier, said the story.

One ploy to lure her within range was a flock of plastic Flamingos and some tempting Flamingo food. However, she actually preferred hanging out with flocks of Canadian geese.

The rescuers twice included energetic canoe paddlers, who once even pushed through ice and slush, The Citizen reported.

On another occasion, said the newspaper, two men in wetsuits readied to nab Eilish only to be foiled by beavers slapping their tails on the water, and inducing her into flight. Ultimately, Canadian residents themselves flocked to Haden Park, said The Citizen, "to gaze at and photograph the area's top tourist attraction as the flamingo feeds in the creek."

Finally, in early December, The Citizen began regular reports about the Flamingo hanging around, resting and feeding in Graham Creek, and becoming a daily capture target for bird rescuers led by Ms. Nihei.

All of Ms. Nihei's, the bird center's and other volunteers' work did ultimately pay off. By this time, this confused Chilean Flamingo was standing on ice, perhaps for the first time in her life. Although perhaps she might have done so back in captivity, if a sudden freeze surprised her caregivers. She now was hungry for underwater creatures and organisms no longer available in the freezing weather.

Three rescuers, including the ever-persistent Ms. Nihei, fearing her permanent disappearance, were elated when two of them first spotted the freezing pink Flamingo. About 30 Flamingo fans watched as the pros stalked the big winged bird. They cheered and took photographs when pursuers finally netted her.

The Citizen reported: "the Anatomy of a Rescue: Dec. 10: At about 12:30 p.m., Elisha returns to Graham Creek and begins wandering slowly in the general direction of the mist net trap. At about 2 p.m., the volunteers creep up to the front of the net as Elisha (again, the name she adopted for Canadians) wanders into the mist-net trap. They pull out the support poles, dropping the net flap and trapping her. Volunteers plunge into the water, grab her, wrap her in a blanket and take her to the centre, to be examined and persuaded to eat as she gets over the shock of her capture. Her adventure in the region and almost 2 ½ months of freedom are over."

A few days later, the newspaper described Ms. Nihei's celebration outfit: a Flamingo pink silk blouse, pink leather shoes and a pair of pink-flecked cotton slacks. She flew about as the Wild Bird Care Center hosted a celebration to thank the "dozens of volunteers" who helped save the famous Flamingo from the Canadian cold.

The bird liberating leader said: "We call it a capture. But, it's funny because in reality, Elisha captured us. In just over a month, she captured our hearts. We are a happy group because we were all in on this."

The adventures of Eilish were indeed news worldwide! The Citizen reported a class of Egyptian fourth grade student sent regular emails into Canada asking what she was up to now. Some local students regularly sent Flamingo drawings in crayon to Ms. Nihei's nature center.

While readying for a commercial airline trip, rather than preparing for her own winged flight back to Connecticut, Eilish waited comfortably in a small room, known as "the tub room." Despite the limited space available, her fans photographed this new media star from all angles.

Ms. Nihei and Michael Bean, then caretaker for the Livingston Ripley Sanctuary, Eilish's home environs, arranged for her to jet back home. It was quite a paperwork preparation with Canadian bureaucrats. Altogether she had six certificates from four levels of government. They included: an export permit, an endangered species release form, a certificate of health, a special hardship exemption to fly directly into Connecticut and finally, a plane ticket, commercial Canadian sponsors purchased to return to her home pond.

The Citizen and two other well-known Canadian businesses paid the freight for Eilish's trip home. Emails from fans flew into sites around Canada wishing Eilish a smooth flight home. Some sweet written greetings were hand delivered into her flight cage. One said: 'Bye Eilish! Have a safe flight home!'

As I was readying to drive home one December 1997 late afternoon from my Hartford Courant reporting duties, a news photographer approached me inside the newsroom. He asked if I could lead a news crew from the Ottawa Citizen back to Litchfield where they were staying overnight. They photographed and wrote about the unique tale of a Flamingo's travels and adventures, he explained.

I was immediately excited because, of course, I had followed the extended story any time I saw it in The Courant or elsewhere. The Ottawa newsman and the photographer and I shook hands before we hopped into our respective cars ready for the bumper to bumper ride to the Litchfield Inn, right around the corner from Eilish's home, and my own.

Once our cars parked in the inn's driveway, I was anxious to converse with the newsmen, obtain some intimate story details, and tell them the Flamingo they were covering was from a sanctuary operated by my blood relatives. After a brief conversation, I volunteered: "If there is anything I can do for you, I will!" Immediately the reporter asked: "What is the name of Eilish's boyfriend?" After my initial surprised silence, I replied: "Oh that is insider information, well beyond my knowledge! But, I'll check."

Reaching home, I became so incredibly curious about those newsmen's upcoming story and photographs the next day, I immediately called them back at the inn to make sure they sent me a copy. As soon as I was on the phone with one of them, I had no chance to speak before he exclaimed: "Hey, we found out who Eilish's boy friend is! His name is Maurice! Isn't that incredible?!"

I was speechless. I knew immediately that name was perfect for their story, readied for the next day. Maurice is a famous, popular Canadian name, if only because the Montreal Canadians' biggest hockey star ever was Maurice "The Rocket" Richard.

The next day, I did not bother to wait for snail mails delivering The Citizen's story from Canada. There it was in all its glory, right on the paper's Internet site. I could not believe it. My eyes became riveted to the screen.

Depicted in a photo is Eilish, just as she entered her home, and met with Maurice.

The Ottawa Citizen's news story created a fictitious, but amusing conversation between the two birds who reportedly were excited about this amazing reunion.

Maurice: "Hey, how are you! You look great!"
Eilish: "You look great too!"
Maurice: "I missed you so much. What's it like up there?"

Eilish: "Really nice. But I haven't been pursued that hard since I met you."

Maurice: "I know, we've been talking about that in group...." (Footnote six)

The rest of that conversation is a bit of an imaginary stretch in an effort to be funny. In it Maurice asks if Eilish met any males on her trip. She responds that she indeed did, and Maurice immediately answers that he is now a lot better male after his sex change operation. Possibly some readers might have laughed hysterically, while others rolled their eyes. (Footnote seven)

Later, I telephoned my cousin, Rosemary Ripley, to find out how these two Flamingo lovers came to be known as Eilish and Maurice. "One of our caretakers, Maurice, had a girl friend named Eilish, and he wanted to know whether he could name a pair of sanctuary Flamingos. I said yes, so they became Maurice and Eilish."

More recently, Ian Gereg, Director of Aviculture and Education at the sanctuary, offered additional historical perspective about Eilish and Maurice. Ian explained: "Dillon's wife, Mary, bought Dillon a group of Chilean flamingos from a defunct auto racing park in Florida as an anniversary present.

There were a total of six or eight when they first arrived in Litchfield. After the last male from the group died in 2007, Eilish was traded for a pair of Southern Screamer ducks to a Virginia zoo to be with other flamingos. There she reached the age of 30 plus, laid her first eggs and hatched her first young (ones)."

That zoo had better clip the young ones' wings regularly, because they probably have Mom's roving DNA! And Eilish's wild flight to Canada, after years of sanctuary confinement, shows beyond any doubt that birds, no matter how domesticated, have the indelible spirit, strength and mental abilities to return to the wild. Certainly, in this case, it was fortunate Eilish got such amazing help from humans, because she was so far away from her home in Chile.

Footnote one alpha:
http://www.google.com/imgres?imgurl=http://www.benhallphoto.com/wp-content/uploads/2009/09/chilean-flamingos-in-flight-over-andes-mountains1.jpg&imgrefurl=http://www.benhallphoto.com/workshops/patagonia-course-2010/&h=298&w=550&sz=88&tbnid=Gey3myjDPmm53M:&tbnh=63&tbnw=117&zoom=1&docid=BTT_XYa-CNt1DM&hl=en&sa=X&ei=L59XT9HPDYfq0gG0n4DMDw&ved=0CC8Q9QEwAA&dur=578

Footnote one: http://articles.courant.com/1997-10-01/news/9710010376_1_flamingos-bird-experts-aviary

Footnote two: http://www.seaworld.org/infobooks/flamingos/fadapt.html

Footnote three: http://www.seaworld.org/infobooks/flamingos/fadapt.html

Footnote four: http://onnaturemagazine.com/kathy-nihei-profile.html

Footnote five: http://www.fpinfomart.ca/news/ar_results.php?q=3825114&sort=pubd

Footnote six: Ottawa Citizen News Story 1997

Footnote seven: The Ottawa Citizen's news stories were crucial in putting together details of the Chilean Flamingo's Canadian rescue for this tale.

Eilish's adventures were extraordinary. But every day, some duck, goose, swan or other flier confronts routine drama with one human or another or even several humans at a time.

Big Daddy Swan Protects His Brood From The Road Runners

As I rode my bike around the hairpin turn near Litchfield High School Sunday, I could not yet see the leaders of Litchfield Hill's famous road race.

What I did see clearly, however, was a pair of white Mute Swans and their four little cygnets, taking it easy on a grassy bank spot close to the road. They were waddling around about two yards from the corner and would not be visible to approaching roadrunners. Several feet below the bank is the small pond where the swans were nesting.

Anticipating trouble, I immediately pointed out the potential problem to a police officer, supervising road race traffic and runners' security. However, the officer immediately replied that there was no way he was going to confront the two potentially dangerous adult Swans. Apparently, he knew from experience how aggressive swans can be while protecting their young.

But the two of us could see that when the road runners made their sharp left turn from the long straightaway to another road leading uphill, they and the swans would be in for a shocking confrontation, just feet away from one another.

So as the first runners rounded that sharp corner, the officer repeatedly yelled out, "Watch out for the swans!" But, the warnings came far too late to avoid trouble. How could the roadrunners even imagine that a family of swans would be standing almost on top of their asphalt race path?

As the first six runners made the turn and rushed past the swan family, only about a foot or two away, Daddy swan was alerted! His neck began pumping back and forth in the emergency. However, initially, the runners came around the turn too abruptly and speedily for Daddy swan to be ready for them.

But, as other runners followed, Mother guarded her babies on the bank to the rear, while Daddy, right next to the roadside, began snipping his beak at the back of unknowing runners' legs. He missed, and then he missed again! But as he became more accustomed to the rhythm of the continuing flow of runners, the swan's big beak came closer and closer to hitting the racers' rear ends or legs as they headed up the hill past the high school.

Finally, Daddy swan got it just right. He ambushed a male runner in a blue and white-striped tracksuit. Big Daddy jumped right out in the road in front of the shocked competitor. Amazingly, the runner narrowly avoided a dangerous collision by pulling his stomach back, throwing up his arms and moving sideways to continue the run. His nearby bare-chested running competitor watched wearily and used a few fast getaway steps to move the rest of the way uphill unimpeded.

Big Daddy Swan attacks a runner during the famous Litchfield Road Race. (Photo By Dennie Williams)

Meanwhile, the police officer moved closer to the male swan. He pulled out a whistle and blew it repeatedly as hard as he could. The aggressive Daddy swan was not impressed. He honked harder than the whistle, and the officer, seeing it was no use, backed off down the road.

If Daddy swan had been a human road race spectator, and threatened a competing runner like that, he would have been arrested for attempted assault by the policeman on the scene. His defense would have been: 'I was simply protecting my wife and kids from a home invader!'

In this situation, Mom swan must have reasoned it made no sense to sit nearby roadrunner danger after danger, and watch her mate confront runner after runner.

Leaving Daddy to continue his macho challenge, she abruptly waddled away with her babies down the bank, and slid with them back into the small pond adjacent to the road.

Minutes later, Daddy got tired of craning his neck and readying attack after attack. Momma and the babies appeared safe now, while churning in the pond, and Daddy must have surmised the flow of runners was never-ending. So he turned away, waddled down the bank and slid into the water near his family, as a new larger group of runners rushed by.

The police officer looked relieved as he stuffed his whistle away in a pocket and walked back toward his cruiser to continue his watch over the festivities.

Even as a lifelong Litchfield, Connecticut, resident, I cannot image any natural spot in the world that can be more of a dream for water birds and nature lovers than Costa Rica.

Here is my concluding poetic-like tale in honor of a wonderful natural habitat for all living beings.

Awesome Birds, Frogs, Snakes, Crocs and Insects Inside The Costa Rican Jungle

It was early sunny morning in beach-infested Manzanillo, Costa Rica, kilometers north of Panama. (Footnote one)

Riding there entailed driving miles down a rocky, pot-holed dirt road,

Almost dead-ending at Maxi's Restaurant-Bar, frequented by fast-drinking beach-goers, surf boarders and swimmers.

It's a roughly built two-story box-like edifice surrounded by roughly hued wood veranda and light brown sandy beach.

Right in the immediately adjacent tiny town, from almost every tree, bush and sagging electric wire,

Came the chant, cluck, song or beak tapping of one bird or another. (Footnote two)

Seemingly, most every other tree

Contained one or more Boat billed flycatchers with black and white masked face,

Light brown back with a yellow breast,

Identical to Bermuda's Yellow Bird, the Great Kiskadee!

But instead of kisadeeing, the winged flier high pitches and low pitches its repetitious notes.

Meanwhile, frogs', croak, croak, croaks and lizards', chirp, chirp, chirps vibrated out from 360 degrees!

Bird sounds, too numerous to recreate, overwhelmed the diminutive town's airwaves.

Tino, a mischievous, talkative middle-aged Afro-Caribbean nature guide for two USA couples

Constantly pointed up into tree leaf masses, identifying bird after bird.

Tourist binoculars sometimes failed to pinpoint what his bare eyes so easily observed right away.

Half way up a bush, mostly half hidden by leaves, was the Scarlet Rumped Tanager,

All black, and yes, a scarlet red rump!

From its perch, the six-inch long bird recurrently high-whistled.

Suddenly it flew up into air. Quickly, it disappeared into the lower brush.

Nonetheless, instant mind cameras captured an amazing, flash

Of scarlet rump belonging to that jet-black bird on the wing.

Next sight spectacular- just like beautiful and hysterical comic book characters!

Up on a high branch appeared a pair of Chestnut-Mandibled Toucans, twenty inches long

With big curved beaks colored yellow, orange and cyan blue, (Footnote three)

Light yellow necks and shimmering black bodies.

Opening wide, the big ones let out high squawk, squawk, squawk, squawk screeches.

Such a unique multicolored, clown-like sight awed tourists who must have scared the birds airborne with people-intense, moving eyeball stares underneath them.

Nearby, a little five-inch Yellow Breasted Flycatcher sounded a sky-high peep, peep, peeyup.

Insects anyone? Plenty out there!

On we sauntered down dusty Peru brown Main Street, just a few walk-steps here and there

Past a few small, wood-brown one or two story aged box-like homes.

No millionaires here!

Constantly, we were on bird alert.

Up on a phone wire, the silhouette of a bitsy Blue-Crowned Marmot with iridescent blue head and long tail.

Its powder blue tail appeared to be a spare, long wing feather, attached loosely to its olive green rear end.

Binoculars magnified the bird's big black beak, black triangles with that iridescent blue around brown eyes, and a light orange breast.

In a bush below the Marmot sat a Scarlet Hepatic Tanager.

Cameras immediately clicked at it from every possible angle.

"The female sings a song similar to the male's, but softer, shorter, and less harsh. She sings in answer to the male's song, and as she is gathering nesting material." (Footnote four)

It must like posing, despite its blushing color. It didn't move, until I tried a close-up photo click. Away it flew!

Regularly, Tino pointed up, up and up to scores of even more radiant, shining colored birds.

Those hosts sang out every note and intonation imaginable.

Their human guests, necks straining upward, were ear and eye riveted.

Out off the lumpy light brown dirt road, we walked toward the ocean.

Cyan Blue sky lightened, as sun pierced cumulus clouds.

Seagulls soared-cried.

Salt-water breezes wafted into ears and noses.

Soooo refreshing!

Onward to the pastel brown sandy beach and light sky-blue ocean!

White-crested waves broke gently with soothing rushing water resonance again, again, again and again.

Little waves, then bigger ones, crashed and soon pulled back out under new big and small ones.

Blue sea became white rolling wakes flattened and spread flat by sand-flowing wet beach.

Coconut trees' leaves created wind-waving triangular green motions above.

Their haunting wrinkled light brown trunks and large splinter leaf shadows permeated the sands below with haunting, moving shadows.

Green or dusty brown or hazy black coconuts hung above or lay stranded underneath tree trunks on the endless sands below.

Looking one way, the long beach curved out toward the ocean and sky.

Back in the opposite direction, the sight of seemingly endless beach was cut off by palm trees, their big striated pea-green leaves blowing up, down and sideways.

Tino guided tourist couples to the target, Gandoca Manzanillo Refuge, "Protecting some the region's most endangered flora and fauna." (Footnote five)

All shoes off, then on again, after we waded in a slow-moving sandy brown mucky jungle stream flowing into the ocean.

The scene then darkened, bit by bit as thick leaved tree tops shrouded the sky.

Huge palm leaves, and smaller leaves of ancient trees so much taller creates uneven, but riveting sky-scapes. Broken clouds and jags of blue sky and sun-rays everywhere, breaking through tree tops.

On the brown dirt path, filled with tree-root systems, deeper we strode.

At the base of a little brown hill covered with brush and trees, we looked far up into the tallest of trees to spot two thin, black brown monkeys, clinging to lengthy vertical slow moving branches.

The Howlers sounded off like the start of a wild windstorm, so loud they can be heard three miles away and are said to be the loudest animal on the planet. Those haunting cries mark their territory. (Footnote six)

Really! At night, the first time those monkey howls vibrate the jungle, sounds like strong wind and heavy rain readying to fell loads of tree limbs.

On a hilltop, Tino's hand abruptly pulled back a dead leaf uncovering a fat brown centipede, its legs wiggling underneath a body-shell.

He quickly placed it in a reluctant male tourist's hand. Seconds later, it crawled off and fell ground ward.

Minutes later, with a chuckle, Tino dared all of us to vibrate one of many rolled up big lime green leafs from Heliconia and Calathea plants, growing vertically straight up, funnels all.

A lady tourist high voiced a "No!" But her hubby soon cupped his hands around a funnel.

Out of the top darted three, four, five little grey-blue fuzzy Leaf-roosting bats!

Startled we all were!

But, it was such fun, we all tried funnel vibrations again and again.

Bats repeatedly went airborne in every direction.

Games over, we walked into thicker jungle!

Soon, Tino slowly pealed back a stemmed yellow green vine.

A tiny bright orange red frog clung to it.

Cameras clicked again.

Seconds later, our photos also captured a coiled tiny gold yellow snake climbing a tree with its 'feet' scales.

Another few steps stationed us behind a huge tree.

We stared up, down and all around into the jungle.

The Monkey Ladder, a thick light grey vine, had hypnotized us. (Footnote seven) Its strands wound all around themselves. They climbed from one tree to the next.

Perfect for "lizards, snakes, sloths to monkeys, the trapeze artists of the forest canopy." (Footnote eight)

Now looking down to ground, ants crawled all over the jungle's floor.

Soldier Army Ants in Peru Brown uniforms swarmed on dead leaves.

Boy, can those little bulbous bodied guys with bent wires for legs bite!

The back of my hand reddened and swelled up from uncontrollable itching.

Scariest was a treed big black Bullet Ant.

If you dare, it fits perfectly between thumb and forefinger.

Tino daringly placed his fingertip next to it.

"It strikes you like a bullet and makes you very sick," he exclaimed.

Like Trojans, an endless stream of Saddle Brown Leaf-Cutter Ants with tiny light-neon bodies crawled in a long line.

Holding delectable tiny little lime green leaf slices, they headed to earth holes, then subterranean nests.

Wow, behind a tree was a series of huge sienna brown, fluffy, large holey anthills. Crawling one to two feet into the air: ants call them SKYSCRAPERS.

We hiked on, as I began profusely sweating.

Into lowland rainforest, a wetland and a mangrove swamp, we trudged.

There, pool-swimming, appeared a small, narrow headed, skinny snouted hazy green crocodile with head popping eyes.

Jungle growth reflected in the pool of water it was gliding through.

Swimming toward it from the other pool end was a cute little baby crocodile.

Nothing on their bodies seemed to move their scaly, armored skin above, even though their own movements rippled the dark swamp directly to the rear of their hindquarters.

As it turns out, these scary swimmers have webbed fingers!

Out of the swampland climbed we, while birds chanted, cawed and peeped,

And tired human necks craned to scan thickets of leaves above, where feathered creatures lurked.

As the two couples and guide began their move out of the jungle, there in a small clearing darted a big Blue Morpho Butterfly!

Its bright neon-blue iridescent wings, framed in black, looked like a miniature spotlight shown right on them.

I ran, ran, and darted everywhere after the flying insect with my camera.

Two shots: no butterfly capture, just boring brown turf and bushes.

The darting blue flier soon evaporated into jungle tangles of brush and greenery. I was stricken to have missed photo-capturing it!

Eventually, the nature refuge's guests slogged back to nearby welcome sunny beaches and refreshing waves.

There, the light blue sky with fluffy clouds, the sounds and water sights soothed weary, but still inspired ears and eyes.

Many pleasant jungle dreams would likely follow days and weeks later.

Footnote one:
http://www.govisitcostarica.com/region/city.asp?cid=394

Footnote two: Based bird songs, colors and descriptions on http://www.naturesongs.com/costa.html" \n _blank

Footnote three: The Cornell Lab of Ornithology http://www.allaboutbirds.org/guide/Scarlet_Tanager/lifehistory/ac

Footnote four: Toucan photo http://www.bugbog.com/images/galleries/costa-rica-pictures/costa-rica-toucan.jpg

Footnote five: http://waynesword.palomar.edu/plmay97.htm#spiraling

Footnote six: Amazon.com at http://images.google.com/images?q=monkey+ladder&oe=utf-8&client=firefox-a&rlz=1R1GGIC_en___US358&um=1&ie=UTF-8&ei=6BprS43CDZTN8Qbk9PSKBg&sa=X&oi=image_result_group&ct=title&resnum=4&ved=0CCIQsAQwAw

Footnote seven: http://waynesword.palomar.edu/plmay97.htm

End

Dennie Williams, the author and a graduate of The Choate School and Middlebury College, is an investigative reporter with five decades of experience. His pen name for news stories is Thomas D. Williams.

Thank you for taking the time to read my book. You may contact me on Facebook or LinkedIn under my name, Dennie Williams. In the event you would like to recommend the book to friends or associates, please tell them a summary is available at www.birdscrittersbutterflies.webs.com/.